(".....All Things Come Of Thee... 1Chr. 29:14)

My Book of:
Sermons, lectures
and Biblical Insights

Hilary H. Battle

Thee of Come Things All...

ISBN 0-9703823-5-9

Copyright 2002 by
Hilary H. Battle
P. O. Box 604131
Cleveland, OH 44104

Published by

LIghtHouse Press
P.O. Box 281375
Nashville, Tennessee 37228

Table of Contents

Preface

This book of sermons and lectures was developed after many years of preaching and lecturing and are my reflections on the Bible and related subjects under discussion. I was inspired by my encounters with people of diverse backgrounds, my travels, studies, and researches. For years I have focused on the areas of counseling, lecturing and preaching on the subjects that are contained in this book. The contents of each chapter emerged after years of experiences; foremost of which was the inspiration I got from studying the Bible.

My approach to developing this book is not to challenge religious thoughts or change anyone's theological interpretations of understanding the Bible, but rather to give my readers an opportunity to consider some of my insights and life experiences. It will also give my readers an opportunity to add their own notes to the subjects discussed. I trust for these reasons this book will be perused in that light.

I take this time now to acknowledge those many authors, commentators and writers that make up my repertoire, for which even if I were conscious of them all, would be impractical and impossible to completely list. Hopefully, this book will serve as an honor and credit to those authors, commentators and writers from whom I have gained many insights. I also acknowledge my family members, especially my wife, Kathy, who forbearingly gave of herself during the completion of this work; the incalculable debt to my sister, Crystal Battle-Hughley (we affectionately call Bunny) my typist, with her dexterity of fingers and eyes of an eagle. I do not claim absolutism in these contents.

My readers, both critics and non-critics, equally honor me for their valued opinions. However, my greatest blessing is from God, from whom I drew strength daily to be inspired and spiritually driven to completion. Finally, with due respect to other versions of the Bible, I chose to quote from the NRSV unless otherwise indicated. Any errors or omissions are completely unintentional.

Hilary H. Battle

Chapter
One

THE BLACKNESS OF THE BIBLE

Song of Solomon 1:5; Exodus 4:6,7

Rationale: The argument for the blackness of the Bible

Topic: A Biblical Attitude Towards Whiteness

The black consciousness surrounding the color of Jesus among black America, surfaced in the mid to late 1960's with the publication of <u>The Black Messiah</u>, Albert B. Cleage, Jr.; and James Cone's <u>Black Theology and Black Power</u>. Since then, many scholarly books have been written on the subject of the blackness of Jesus, black Christianity, and the black presence in the Bible.

My presentation today is not so much in the area of the above topics, for each is a definitive study within itself, but is rather centered on the attitude of the people of the Bible towards the color white. What I will attempt to address tonight, is what the people of the Bible thought about the color white. For we know that the language of the people reflects, in general, who they are; their character, their values, their belief systems, social taboos and their prejudices. Hence, the topic:

A BIBLICAL ATTITUDE TOWARDS
THE COLOR WHITE.

As black people in America, we need to know how very important it is to keep alive our historical and religious experiences. We need to immerse ourselves more into the positive experience and productive contributions of our heritage and history by focusing on, who is really who in history and who were those people in the Bible that gave the Lord such a hard time. Yet, when we do this we need

1

to guard against social ethnocentrism and religious exclusivism which, in time, will develop into black racism. It was Martin Luther King who once said, "Black racism is just as evil as white racism." Yet, we can begin learning more about ourselves in history and religion by first understanding how the behavior of Western societies have shaped our understanding against people-of-color.

American literature is so deeply stained with color consciousness that history as well as religion, as we know it, has been heavily tainted with Euro-centric ideologies. If we add to this the fact that American histories and religions have been radically altered by white racist writers, then we end up with libraries filled with books void of the historical and religious contributions made by people-of-color in America. In other words, in Western society, a person's color has a lot to do with their place in history. The more colored they are, the more likely they have no place in Western history. W.E.B. DuBois succinctly said; "The problem with the 20th century is the color line"[1] while the white historian, Herbert Aptheker in his book, Afro-American History, expanded on this quote by writing: "*Every aspect of (the American history up to and including 1970...everything, absolutely everything...that has ever appeared or ever occurred in the United States of America must be understood in terms of the relationship thereto of the Black people in the United States. [and] To the degree that...the historiography (of that period) is false and is racist.*"[2] In other words, in America as well as in all European society, Western historians and theologians have a problem with crediting people-of-color with any positive contributions they have made to the human family. Even today, written experiences about our contributions to the

---

1 H. Aptheker, Afro-American History, p. 55.
2 Ibid, p.14.

2

world of human existence, must be screened by our black professional historical and theological vanguards. In that way blackness in the history and religious books of Americans will not be relegated to just the color of the ink used to print the pages in the books.

Thus, black people need to develop new attitudes towards the colors of black and white in order to be able to perceive these colors through eyes of other than those of Western ideologies. We can start, by studying the historical attitudes of this country towards the colors black and white to discover how these attitudes influence our understanding in everything. What must be seriously considered is, the greatest influence imposed upon the mind of a people comes by means of their religion. For example, religious influence imposed upon us by means of hundreds of years of traditions has caused us to associate white with purity, joy and happiness; and black with death and sadness. Who would dare think of wearing white to a funeral or black to a wedding? But I ask the question, what difference does it make other than being victims of religious traditional trappings?

What we must consider when it comes to the issues of black and white, is that early in life we learn color associations. One need only look in any dictionary under the definitions of black and of white and they will immediately notice the sharp contrast between them. In other words, white in Western civilization symbolizes all things good, while black symbolizes all things evil.

A negative effect of these attitudes against blackness took place as early as the Dred Scott case in American history. From this case, blackness and its negative impact on the American scene, left a nasty yet permanent scar on the minds of all America. History records that a slave named Dred Scott accompanied his army officer master to the slave free state of Missouri and lived there for 30 years on free soil. Under the historical document, 'The Missouri Compromise' of 1830, blacks were freed from slavery while living in Missouri. Missouri would only join the United States if they could remain a slave free state. The case of Dred Scott was simple. Why should he be a slave in a free territory?

Dred Scott's argument went to the Supreme Court, which clearly ruled against his freedom and demanded that he remain a slave forever. The slave laws of the U.S. did not guarantee his freedom in a free territory. The court's argument for Scott remaining a slave, in a slave free territory, was based on constitutional grounds. The court argued that the founding fathers of the land had never intended African people to be part of; "WE THE PEOPLE..." as stated in the Constitution. Therefore, in the court's final decision, the fate of this nation's negative attitudes towards blacks was sealed in the minds of white America. For in the infamous words of Chief Justice Roger Taney, of the Supreme Court, "...Blacks have no rights that white men are bound to respect..."[3] The Supreme Court ruled from this argument in 1857, that no black, free or otherwise could ever claim U.S. citizenship.

Such a decision reinforced in the minds of white America, negative attitudes already at work against the color black in general. It further licensed whites in America, to think whether anti or pro-black, that black people by nature are inferior to whites and thus by law, white people can practice racism legally without reprisals from the law.

---

3 R. D. Heffner, A Documentary History of The United States, p. 131.

We also learned during the early development of European attitudes towards the color black, that blackness stood in sharp contrast with their own color. In a sense, color precipitates behavior of self towards others. Color also reveals much about the attitudes of a people who in turn use color associations to negatively characterize the other.

For example, if white is perceived as good and black as evil, then one can accurately assume that the dominate color of the people in that society who fosters such notions are themselves white. On the other hand, if black is perceived as good and white evil, then one can equally surmise that the dominate color of a people in that society who fosters such notions are themselves black. Therefore, it would appear that there is a preconceived correlation in the minds of people between one's color and their behavior. It would further be assumed that the reason why some people act the way they act is because of their color. In other words, anyone whose color is different from mine would naturally have a behavior different from me. And of course, in order not to incriminate my color, their behaviors would naturally be inferior to mine. Thus, anyone who thinks like this would naturally assume that one's behavior is a result of one's color.

Color also seems to predict how one treats the other. Winthrop Jordan, in his book White Over Black, made this observation; "...white and black [implies] opposites. It connotes purity and filthiness, virginity and sin, virtue and baseness, beauty and ugliness, beneficence and evil, God and the devil."[4]

To stretch this notion, we discover that the ultimate Being of the universe, God, is always portrayed in the likeness of

4 W. Jordan, White Over Black, p.7.

5

the people themselves. Their understanding of good takes on the color of their God, who in turn takes on the color of the people's image of their God. Thus, to the American Indians, God is red, and red is good; to the Asian Budda, God is gold, and gold is good; to the Europeans, God is white and white is good; and to the African God is black, thus black is good. Therefore, how one treats the other, can in fact be justified, by one's religious beliefs and their religious teachings, by means of association. One will use self as a standard of good. Thus, whatever their color, then God is that same color. If, therefore, God is good and they are created in the image of God, then they also must be good.

Yet, and for the most part, the religious understanding of the color of the people in the Bible is not understood to most black Americans, that all the characters of the Bible are people-of-color. What must be considered is this: (*there are not black people found in the Bible every now and then, but rather the whole content of the Bible is of and about people-of-color*). Now, this is neither good nor bad, but it is germane to how we identify spiritually with the Bible to aid us in our spiritual growth. Yet, the reason we struggle with this issue is that most, if not all of our encounters with religious figures in the Bible have been presented to us as being white. Therefore, our general understanding of the Bible has become tainted with subtle themes of Western Literary denigration of the color black. In other words, when blacks are featured in the Bible, they are featured in subservient roles opposite leading white characters. We struggle to overcome this image of the oppressor being the same color of the God we worship. Yet, we fail to speak out against this type of imagery because we already have an insalubrious understanding of the color black long before we are introduced to the Bible.

We never bother to question why it is that we are featured in subservient roles in the Bible; such as slaves to whites, burden bearers and servants. We approach these contradictions in silent denial. We do this by deeming it theological unnecessary and unimportant to know what color people of the Bible really are, because we do not consider such notions as being important to our salvation.

Yet, our silence on the issue of the blackness of the Bible acts to reinforce our existing biblical attitudes on this issue. For Western religious thoughts and writings are predominately white and do not bother to include on its theological agenda the notions of any people in the Bible being any color other than white. Hence, to most black people, as said in the words of Gunnar Myrdal, in his book An American Dilemma, "God and the angels are ordinarily white to Negroes as they are to all white churchgoers...therefore it is senseless to think otherwise."[5] Thus, the problem with many black people is that when we read the Bible, we read whiteness as being the normal color of the people of the Bible and we struggle hunting for the black presence in the Bible.

Yet, the irony of it all is built into the response of black people. For we do not question the whiteness of the Bible or that of Jesus, but we do question the blackness of the Bible and that of the blackness of Jesus. Only in America can Jesus be accepted to be any color without question except black and that the greatest time spent in defending the color of Jesus is when He is featured, as a black man.

Thus, Western civilization has in every area influenced our understanding, perceptions and interpretation of the Bible.

---

5 G. Myrdal, An American Dilemma, Vol. II, p. 866.

Western civilization has succeeded in doing this simply by our unquestioned acceptance of Western theologies and religious publications flooding our black churches. We, without question accept 'in toto' the Bible's interpretations of: Cook Publishing Company, Moody Bible Literature, Unger's Bible Handbook, Guidepost Literature, American Bible Society Publications, Zondervan Publications, the KJV, and the list goes on.

We in turn have either rejected, ignored or do not know about the theologies of: Martin Luther King, James Cone, Edward Blyden, F.M. Snowden, Jr., Samuel Samkage, Richard Allen, Bishop Turner, L.R. Jones, Albert B. Cleage, Allen Boesak, Charles V. Hamilton, Gayraud S. Wilmore; nor do we even know much about our church fathers before us who felt the bitter chastening rod in the days when hope for them had died, so that our weary feet could enjoy this place for which they could only sigh.

Even more, what we must remember about American religion is, almost every important theological interpretation of the Bible along with religious archaeological findings, take their beginnings in Europe and white American long before black people have access to them. Black people get the finished products of Western religions, not the raw findings. What we must realize is that interpretations take place on the discovery level by the discoverer. Black access to the discovery level is practically non-existing. Also, what is extremely important is, the divine revelation made to the minds of the original writers of Scripture is seldom, if ever considered. *In other words, what does scripture mean to the people who wrote the Bible? Not only that, but what revealed insights can you and I discover, should we allow the original writers of the scripture to speak to us in accordance with what they wrote and not in accordance with what we read between the lines?*

Thus, for these reasons, we need to approach American histories and theologies with a degree of intellectual caution. We must keep in mind that western literature has negatively impacted our understanding of religion. Western literature, time and again, has proven historically to have little to nothing to do with the black experience.

To sum it up, any finished product in theology and history which has been finished and refined by the pens of a historically proven race of people who interpret all that is black as denigrating, must be approached by all black people with some degree of intellectual suspicion and caution. Such literature must first be put to the reality test to see if it fits our cause. Therefore, in light of the notion that blacks are caught-up in the webs of finished theologies and histories spun off the looms of Western literary intellects, coupled with the fact that we do not have pristine access to theological or historical raw materials, we need to explore the Bible for ourselves in an attempt to discover through study and revelation, what it has to say about itself. We need to explore for ourselves *A Biblical Attitude Towards Whiteness.*

EXPLORING BIBLICAL ATTITUDES TOWARDS THE COLOR WHITE

What are Biblical attitudes towards whiteness in the Bible? First, we need to consider how the early Romans and Greeks associated Christianity with black people in their first encounter with the religion of Christianity. All Christianity the Romans encountered was from their encounters with black people.

9

For example, prior to the Greek/Roman encounter with Christianity, Greeks first were known to be religious (Acts 17:22). As a matter of fact, they were observers of many religions (23) in their cities which were "full of idols"(16). In other words, they were addicted to worshiping gods, yet were not in any way knowledgeable of the religion of Christianity (18,23b). Their associations of Christianity with black people as it was introduced to the Roman and Greek empires came about in Acts 13:1: "There were prophets and teachers, Simeon, called black and Lucius from Africa…" Paul himself was even mistaken to be an African in Acts 21:37, 38; but corrected this mistake in identity by saying that he was a Jew. In other words, for a Jew to be mistaken to be an African means both were black. Frank M. Snowden, Jr., writes; "…the early Christians used the Ethiopian as a prime motif in the language of conversion and as a means to emphasize their conviction that Christianity was to include all mankind. That the Ethiopian was so used was a natural development of classical tradition, for the Ethiopian was in many ways a convenient symbol of certain patterns of Christian thought."[6] Thus, we learn from this that black people appeared frequently in early Christian interpretations as a standard of Christianity. Said another way, by the time of Christ, black people were not only widespread throughout the ancient world of religion, but they were an acceptable and notable part of the total ancient known world.

For instance, an early Christian interpretation of the book, Song of Solomon (SOS) is an interpretation of Christ's love for the church. *But, it is also a study of how ancient people avoided the use of the color white due to the preponderance of black people.* For example: SOS reads, "I am black and beautiful" (1:5) as opposed to I am white and beautiful.

---

6 F.M. Snowden Jr., <u>Blacks In Antiquity</u>, p.196.

Black therefore, is a widespread standard of beauty in the ancient world. In fact, color is a standard of reverence, "I am a *rose* of Sharon, a *lily* of the valleys" (2:1).

<u>Something about SOS</u>
SOS does not have any religious content corresponding to that of the other books of the Bible with the exception of Esther. Rather, it is a book of an expression of the epitome of a love relationship between a man and a woman. Therefore, it is a book that is a collection of extraordinary beautiful love poems between lovers. It is a book, which expresses these love poems in a language of color descriptions, void of anything being described in the color white. Said another way, the color white is not mentioned at all in this book. **NOTE:** [SOS 5:10 KJV uses white]. The Hebrew word tsach, (TSAKH) means dazzling, sunny or radiant or shining: RSV, it is radiant and ruddy: KJV, uses white and ruddy. Ruddy is red. The point to be made, is one red and white at the same time? No! for tsach means radiant, not white. Furthermore, all references to love, body parts, a person's character, their feelings, etc., are all described in colors or compared with elements and things having color. The color white is not at all characteristic to the vocabulary of this writer.

Yet, we can go back much further in time than Song Of Solomon. We learn that the first experience with white and the use of white in the Bible is introduced in the book of Genesis.

This first experience with white in the Bible is with Laban. His name means white [Laban, (LAW-BAN) means white in Hebrew]. Laban is a name associated with deception and treachery. Deception existed between Jacob and Laban in that infamous contract involving the speckled and spotted sheep. Laban had taken the opposite sex of each animal species and took them with him in the night, leaving Jacob with sheep and goats that could not breed. In Laban's case he had nothing to lose because he was made to be wealthy at the hands of Jacob's labor of seven years. His same sex sheep did not hurt his wealth, in spite of the fact that they could not breed.

In an earlier instance, Laban did another deceptive thing. He had given Leah to Jacob to marry instead of Rachael whom Jacob was initially promised. This was a clear act of deception on the part of Laban, (Gen.29:25). Jacob in turn had to work for Laban another seven years for Rachael. Laban in turn received another seven free years of labor from Jacob. Yet, this is not all. For we read in Gen.31:41 that Jacob had accused Laban of undermining him ten times in twenty years pertaining to deceptive incidents as these. Hence, Laban a personal name, is cast as a character type. Instead of one having a black character, one has a white character that is associated with deception and treachery.

Again and again in the Bible, whiteness is just as often if not more, seen as a symbol to dread or avoid. Whiteness in the Bible has a reoccurring association with sin or punishment and is a color often feared as a color to avoid. Further examples are found in Exodus, Numbers, 2 Kings, Matthew, Acts and Revelation. In Exodus 4 and Numbers 11, white is featured as a color to be feared. It is perceived as an unnatural skin color as in the cases of; Moses, Miriam, Gehazi and some New Testament events. For instances:

I. The Moses Event in Exodus 4:6
Moses' hand turned leprous as snow. Leprous, Hebrew

tsara, (TSAW-RAH) means scourge. In this instance, God was showing Moses that He could bless him, as he was (black) or punish him if necessary, if he disobeyed by making him Laban (white), by means of tsara. Tsara is leprosy, which turns the skin white. By turning Moses white, he would be easily identified as a sinful man who disobeyed God. This is whiteness as a result of *disobedience*.

II. The Miriam Event in Numbers 12:10:
The Divine indictment against Miriam was that she became leprous. Miriam and Aaron, out of envy, challenged Moses' unique relationship to God. In turn, Miriam turned white. Aaron, in his fear of the same punishment, pleaded to Moses that such a "sin" not be upon him and Miriam. He continued his plea for Miriam that she be not as one "dead," because she had turned "white as snow." Here, whiteness is associated with death as a result of *envy*.

III. The Gehazi Event in 2Kings 5:
This event does not symbolize any good end…only a constant reminder of the continued punishment of God being visited upon a nation of people. Gehazi inherited a transgenerational punishment that would permanently leave on him the badge of greed. Because of his greed, the punishment of leprosy, which was upon Naaman is now upon Gehazi and "unto his descendants forever." This is whiteness as a result of *greed*.

IV. In the N.T.
Whiteness is associated with death, the grave and tombstones as found in Matt. 3:27; "Woe to you, scribes and Pharisees, hypocrites! For you are like whitewashed tombs…" Acts 23:3; "Then Paul said to him, [Ananias, high priest in Rome], God shall strike you, you

whitewashed wall!" This is a whiteness pertaining to the whiteness of dust, tombs and embalming. Rev. 6:8; "And I [John] saw, and behold, a pale horse, and its rider's name was Death, and Hades followed him;" This is a whiteness pertaining to paleness which in turn symbolizes death, Hades and the Destroyer.

Example after example in biblical language is testimony to the fact that the color white was not a natural color of the times to the people of the Bible, that it was uncharacteristic of their culture. It would also appear that the physical location or geography in which one lives, bears heavily upon how they color label things and other people peculiar to their environment. People of ancient warm and tropical climates did not frequently come in contact with snow as an element characteristic to their environment. Hence, anything white was grouped in a category opposite anything of color. These perceptions do not differ from modern day European thought, in that anything of color is grouped in categories opposite anything white. What we learn is, there is a unique kinship between people in similar geographical locations and how they associate character, attitude and things with color.

Color, furthermore, assigned to a people was used as a description of their character, attitude, moods and behavior: And, how a people color code the other is a direct reflection of their own color. Moods, attitudes, character, behavior and personal biases of others are color-coded. For examples:
- One can feel blue, when they are depressed.
- One is yellow, if they scare easily.
- One is washed white as snow when they are free of sin;
- Yet, one's soul is black, if it is infested with sin.
- One turns red when they blush, yet white as a ghost

when they are frighten.

- One has a green thumb if they have a knack for gardening.
- They are brown-nosing, if they are kind-hearted; and when they are in love, their eyes sparkle like diamonds, with lips of cherry red.

Finally, what we have discussed is that white is not a characteristic color in the language of the Bible. Whenever it is used it is as a color descriptive of Divinity as well as a color to be avoided. For instance: Transfiguration, in Mk.9:3, or as death or sin in Matt.23:27. In some instances it is used as an opposite: Matt.5:36, "...you cannot make one hair white or black," ...or a color of description as the description of a coriander seed to describe manna (Ex16:31). It is in few cases used as furniture and floor color and garments mixed with other colors, as in Esther 1:6; 8:15.

What we can conclude from the above is, should one argue against the Bible being a book written by, about and for people-of-color, then one must look closely at the use of language association not only with white but with all colors in the Bible.

Yet, what else must be strongly considered, is the color black in the Bible. We learn that in the Bible, there is no frequent use of black being associated with sin. What we must consider is, of the 26 times that the color black or any form of black is mentioned in the Bible, only 18 are specific to the color black. Of these 18 specific uses of black, at no time is the color black directly associated as being a condition of sin. What we do discover about the relationship of black in the Bible, is that it is associated with; sorrow, gloom, the mood of a person, or it is used as a description of sky, a person's hair, or a garment to be worn. In Revelation, black is used as a description of righteous judgment.

Black slaves in America must have known by spiritual revelation, that in the Bible, the Bible itself refused to condemn its own image. And black slaves must have known that they were created in the image of God, for they did not associate their blackness with oppression, self-hatred, or evil. For when they sang spiritual songs like *Steal Away To Jesus,* the black slave's perception of his slave master, comes out in this verse:

Green trees are bending...Poor sinners stand
a trembling...
The trumpet sounds within-a my soul...I ain't got long
to stay here...

This verse was known to any slave: That *green trees are bending* simply meant; that the white slave masters were in fact bending under the weight of their own avarice, greed and wickedness while carrying the rod of oppression. To the slave, these slave masters stood like healthy *green trees,* bending under the burden of their wickedness. In the eyes of the poor black slave sinner, who stood trembling at the awesome sight of the white oppressor, the slave masters looked like powerful green giants. For the slave associated whiteness with all that was evil.

Therefore, to escape the wrath of the oppressor, the slave's only hope was to escape to freedom which sounded like *A Trumpet Within-a My Soul.* And, when the time came, he knew that there was a way being made for his escape through the Underground Railroad...and one thing for sure, whether he made it or not, lived or died, His Mind Was Made Up To Escape The Inhuman Conditions Of Slavery. Thus, in great jubilation, he would sing in closing,

I Ain't Got Long To Stay Here! And just as the black slave fought to free himself from the wretched conditions of slavery, today we must fight to free ourselves from western biblical aberrations. For we are of the image of God!

February 17, 1998

Chapter Two

MANHOOD

Genesis 2: 4-23

Sociologically, man has been known as many things; God's image, lord of creation, a god in ruins, the aristocrat amongst animals, the most intelligent of animals and the most silly, nature's sole mistake, etc... Yet, however goodly and sophisticated some of these titles may sound they still fall short of the mark of a true man, if compared with the Bible. Some of these titles may even leave a lifetime scar on his manhood. But in the Bible, the woman plays an important part in his coming-of-age into manhood more so than of the social climate of the times. Thus, from a biblical point-of-view, the introduction of woman into the life of man, as recorded in Genesis 2:5-8, supplies a major part of the ingredient for the completion (wholeness/wholesomeness) of his manhood.

With this in mind, to look completely to the world of sociology for the definition of manhood may give us some historical and cultural insights into the plight of man; but sociology, to the exclusion of theology, will not address in toto the meaning or the experience of the coming-of-age into manhood. Thus, to depend solely on the sociological approach in defining manhood, one will discover that sociology contributes little to nothing to his moral and spiritual transforming experience. For sociology does not possess those spiritual transforming ingredients which changes him into a sensitive, caring, responsive and responsible spiritually awakened being. Sociology does not provide man with a spiritual foundation. His spiritual awakening, the most important ingredient in his transformation period into manhood, comes by means of divine intervention.

God provides this divine intervention for man by means of a *fit* woman.

Hence, the coming about of these transforming experiences in the life of a man are not found in the world of sociology but rather in the revelatory words of God "...a helper *fit*[1] *for him*..." as described in Genesis 2.

[Fit: Italics are my emphasis variously translated from the Hebrew word neged, which means; meet, part opposite, counterpart or mate. This is the word chosen by God to describe man's helper. This word, neged along with the Hebrew word azar, means; to protect, aid or surround, together joins to give completeness to Adam. Various translations of the combinations of these words are: Help meet, helper, as his partner, suitable helper, etc. A literal translation would read something like the following: A counterpart who protects, an aid that is part opposite, or mate who surrounds or aids. However, in every case, Eve is cast in a supportive and protective role over against Adam. Furthermore, should this expression be read in context with verses 20, 21, one will also discover that the idea of a marriage relationship consist of two persons exclusively "fit" for each other. Hence, in this paper I will understand "fit," to convey all of the above. For "fit" provides the spiritual awakening ingredient in man which completes his wholeness/wholesomeness.]

Fit, serves a twofold purpose. It is not only used as a means provided by God which blossoms man into full manhood, but *fit* also best describes the nature and character of a specific woman, fit for a specific man. A *fit* woman is the instrument of man's transforming experience

---

1 Translated "meet" in KJV

into manhood. All of this is contained in the expression "...a helper *fit* for him..."

Yet, we must consider something else. What must further be considered is the character of the woman in the creation account of Genesis 2:18. Her character is not to be confused with the character of the female found in the creation account found in Genesis 1:27. Azar[2] (helper), in 2:18 occupies a lower strata of Divine representation, even to the extent of being more representative of the nature and character of man whom "the Lord God formed...from the dust of the earth." Tselem, in 1:27 is the nature and character of man created, "in the image of God." Tselem[3] (image), therefore, occupies a much higher strata on Divine level of things in that it is meant to represent God, not man. Therefore, in the Genesis 1:27 account of creation, one can conclude that included in the meaning, "*in the image of God,*" God uses Himself as the standard of measure for the character of sinless manhood. In the Genesis 2:7 account of creation, this writer does not see the Adam and Eve you and I have come to know so well as being created in the image of God, but rather being formed from the "*dust of the ground.*"

There is, therefore, in the Genesis 2 account a fit likeness of them as they were made from the earth and rather designed for each other. Only in the Genesis 1:27 account of creation, before sin entered the picture, is there a likeness of humanity with the image of God. Genesis 2 does not share this notion. Eve was made to be a helper for Adam whom God formed from the dust. Adam's image is of the earth (3:19), not of God. That is why we are commanded by God to not use any part of the earth to

---

2 Azar; to aid, surround, helper
3 Tselem; illusion, resemblance, a representative figure or image

make an image of Him (Ex.20:4). The image of God is not anything of the earth or of anything He made out of the earth. Hence, our image cannot be associated with the image of God. Furthermore, Eve was made to correspond to Adam, not to God. Eve was made to be fit for Adam, not for God.

Thus, the Adam and Eve in Genesis 2:18 are not the image of God but is rather dust from the earth (3:19) being sustained by the Spirit of God (2:7). In light of this, man and woman are made to fit each other and not made to fit the image of God. They were made by the hand of God, but are not the created image of God (further discussed below in this chapter). Hence, the fitness of woman has relativity to her design for being specifically fit for a specific man. This simply means that every woman of the dust, is not fit for every man of the dust while on the other hand, the dust of the earth is not a fit image of God. Thus, dust has specificity with humankind, not the Spirit. Flesh and Spirit are not the same.

Furthermore, *fit* also fulfills the role of being the extension of man's desires as well as being his moral consciousness. This specially designated term *"...a helper fit for him..."* thrust womankind into the role of being the alter ego for mankind, his out-of-the-body agitator. She is his wake-up call unto manhood. Yet, the phrase, "in the image of God he created them," enters the union at the point where she becomes a fit member of the union (further discussed below in this chapter).

This awakening experience of man's likeness to God comes by means of her fitness to the union. Her fitness for man not only brings harmony to the union but gives him pause to model his manhood after the image of his Creator by means of the harmony she brings to the union. The spiritual implication of this image of God and harmony is found in Paul's second letter to the Corinthians where he wrote, "Do not be mismatched..." (6:14). Thus, this *"fit helper,"* robed in the garment of Adam's *"...bone of my bones, flesh of my flesh..."* becomes the image of God inasmuch as she is the one and only fit helper for that specific union. Harmony of any union is key to the image of God. Therefore, this is the only true mate for man, which acts to awaken him unto a moral conscious and spiritual being called man. His manhood comes full cycle only inasmuch as *"a helper fit for him,"* and *"the image of God"* is united as one in a specific union. In light of this approach, the two expressions are not separates in a marriage, for *"the image of God"* is contained within the harmony of the union as she strives to model her *"fit"* role, after Prov.31: 10ff in ways Christians strive to model their life after Jesus.

But we have a problem. It is a problem of relationship selections, which become improper attitudes toward mate selections. These improper attitudes towards mate selections are deeply rooted in the behavior patterns of our Western culture. Simply put, men and women in our American culture are not properly taught right relationships toward one another. Furthermore, they do not know much about the duty bound spiritual relationship they are to have for one another before they marry. Too much of our learning about male/female relationships is arbitrarily and haphazardly picked-up as we go along the road of life.

Other learned attitudes about relationships have been grafted into us by our parents. We first observe how our parents relate one to another. From them we learn our first lessons in human relationship. Somewhere in between the time our male/female hormones 'kick in' and before we settle down into the serious business of seeking our mates, many of our patterns of behaviors, attitudes, worldviews, mood swings, personalities and how we relate to others are already deeply ingrained in us by our parents. We are more victims of our parent's bad attitudes and negative behaviors than we are products of their wisdom. We in turn mingle these behaviors with our own personal brand of arbitrarily learned mate selecting behaviors. Our mates, in turn, do the same. The consequences are that all relationships are preloaded with our parental imposed behaviors and our own self-serving egos. The results are that relationships come preloaded with everybody's own personal brand of mate expectations.

This method of mate selection is damaging to relationships. It's damaging because it draws its understanding on how to establish a relationship from the societal level of mate selection by means of expectation and parental imposed behaviors and not from duty bound spiritual relationships. Furthermore, personal expectations do not equip couples with tools of understanding. It takes an understanding heart to realize the importance of re-tooling minds with new behaviors when passing from the status of being single to that of the status of a union. What is not realized in a relationship is that what is workable for single persons, may not be workable in a union. Mates must learn anew: Roles, duties and new behaviors while modifying old behaviors and getting rid of bad habits in order to survive a relationship. Furthermore, non-agreed upon unspoken contracts in relations and premature expectations have no place in unions. Why? Because they create problems. In other words, the real you ought to step forth in the courtship, not in the marriage.

Couples must learn to part with their single-person behaviors. Hanging on to past behaviors, which netted them so much while single, can be extremely damaging in a union. Genesis has a lesson for us to learn in that "*a man leaves his father and his mother and cleaves to his wife.*" This leaves something to be learned in the business of <u>leaving</u> and <u>cleaving</u> in that both men and women must learn to leave behind their own past self-serving rules and cleave to God's rules. In other words, all the baggage that you did not cleave to in the courtship, leave it out of the marriage. And all the baggage you may have lugged around while single, unload it before you marry.

Yet, couples make mistakes. One big mistake is their many frustrating attempts to preserve their single-person behaviors while paired in a union. The foundations for their mistakes are laid during the courtship years, because they do all the wrong things during courtship, in preparation for marriage.

First, they spend too much time trying to artificially impress their lover. They spend too much time on mate selecting based on fulfilling each other's personal expectations. They do this in order to secure an anticipated self-gratifying favorable outcome from the relationship.

Secondly, dating persons go through a number of trial and error relationships in attempts to find the one person whom they feel will fit within the boundaries of their single-person behaviors. Simply put, if one relationship does not work try another. Eventually, by mere chance, they may happen upon someone, they feel, at the moment, is their "*fit*" ideal of a mate. They call it love, but it is not love. Rather, it is the pleasure of the bootie not the performance of marriage duty.

Thirdly, should a union be formed from this trial and error attempt, what is eventually discovered is that the union was not rooted in the love model of God's ideal of a *"fit helper."* What they thought to be the ideal love model of God, was only a pairing-up of the behaviors of two single persons playing up to the expectations of the other in order not to lose what they thought is a good thing, or is the real thing. Needless to say, all else that follows are problems and conflicts. What is not immediately realized or even considered is that the relationship will begin to imperceptibly unfold into the world of reality, catching them both unprepared.

But we need to explore more fully from a biblical viewpoint, the contributions a *"fit"* Godly woman makes to the total scheme of manhood. And we can best begin from the premise that in the divine order of things a man without a wife is not complete within himself, no more than manhood without womanhood makes up a complete humanity. Needless to say that the reverse of this premise is also true but, whatever else is said of woman, be it ancient or modern, she alone coupled with the divine act of God working in and through her, completes the full being of man. For what becomes for man the transforming experience in his life that changes him seemingly from a stupor, apathetic, unattached and unemotional animal naming being into a truly conscious, mindful, sensitive, alert, warm congenial and spiritual being, is that of the virtuous (model) woman Proverbs talks about. It has been said among the American Indians that when a man is accompanied by his wife he comes in peace. Thus, the Godly wife, the *"fit"* helper, is his transforming agent of mercy and consciousness that makes him responsive, caring and accountable. Through her, man becomes a peaceful coexisting creative moral and spiritual being. Not just any woman; but 'ishsah.' She is that special woman designed exclusively for 'ish,' which according to Adam, is *"bone of my bone, flesh of my flesh,"* and according to God, the *"fit"* (Azar) helper.

Therefore, to consider the meaning of manhood is to consider Genesis. And to consider Genesis is to consider woman, 'ishsah' and her total role in the design of manhood. It is to consider her as being a part of the ordered universe from the very beginning. In other words, wives, if your man is acting up while living with you, before you 'kick him to the curb,' you need to check out your own 'fitness' record according to God's standards. Furthermore, women need to keep in mind that their understanding of fitness is not limited only to their sexual promiscuity; but, rather expands to include their total behaviors as expressed in Proverbs, *"A foolish woman is noisy: She is wanton and knows no shame,"* (9:13). It is because of this type behavior in womankind, that it is better for a man to *"live in a corner of the housetop than in a house shared with a contentious woman"* (21:9). Thus, from a biblical point-of-view, we must remember that a woman is equally accountable for her bad behaviors and nasty attitudes as she is for her sexual promiscuity or whorish ways. In the Bible, both are treated as being equally destructive to the morals and spiritual well being of any man. A woman can kill his motivation. Simply put, a woman can destroy a man from both ends of her body; her head and her tail; and though this is a harsh indictment against womankind, it is a behavior that has been with us since the beginning of the human experience.
Yet, there are many other contributions a Godly woman

makes to all humanity, which are too often excluded from the overall experiences of manhood. I suppose the very use of the word <u>manhood</u> contributes much to that exclusion. There exists the convenience of selected exclusiveness in the word manhood because it has a twofold designator. It can be applied to both the entire human family or to the male only. Yet, there exist a third implication of exclusion. This exclusiveness is seen in the word manhood because the female presence in the word is absent all the time. In the back of our minds when we use manhood, womanhood is and is not implied at the same time. However, in the word womanhood, manhood is forever contained [Wo(manhood)]. Thus, it would appear that womanhood, was meant to count for something of significance in the original event of manhood simply because even in the beginning the same containment is true. He is 'ish' and she is 'ishsah.' Hence, only together and united is there a completeness to the whole human event. Maybe this same idea of completeness is further conveyed in the Hebrew word 'Azar' (helper). It conveys a meaning of total encompassing. But in a world of sin, the idea of wholeness, completeness and unity between male and female became lost.

Sin caused disunity between male/female. Because of sin, the intended wholeness in a relationship is not brought to the unions. Hence, the full measure of her role to bring harmony to relationships "...*where sin abounds...*" is not fully realized. What is supposed to be realized as relationships of harmony is now heavily tainted with sin. Under these circumstances, any contribution she brings to the marriage relation is at best quite nebulous, insignificant, conflicting, opposing, confusing, controversial, competitive and contentious. At worse, she makes no significant contributions to the harmony of relationships, or to the institution of manhood. Sin does not unify – it disunites. A union in sin will strip a man of his manhood because sin does not recognize wholeness.

But though her contribution to our manhood at times may be downplayed, her role, she being a Godly woman [and I cannot overemphasize Godly woman] is nevertheless not diminished from our experiences as men. She, being faithful to her divine role, weighs heavily upon her ability as a woman to significantly contribute to our roles as men. According to the divine order of things, she is by God, placed in such a position in the human experiences as having first opportunity of a nurturing mother, who applies precisely the proper dosage of moral and spiritual cultivation to all humanity so as the human family will not fall into total immorality. For just as God placed Adam in the garden of Eden to cultivate it to keep it from going wild, woman was placed into the life and experiences of man so as he would not succumb to total degeneracy. Thus, I believe Genesis records the importance of this role women have in maintaining that delicate balance which exist between spiritual cultivation and degeneracy in humanity. In turn, we must study the rich insights afforded us by Genesis on the meaning of manhood. Otherwise, we may run the risk of forfeiting the rich resources of our manhood heritage and end up like those hapless souls in Romans 1.

But, we must consider the intended crowning glory of God's creation. Woman was to be the best of His creation. She, unlike Adam, never touched dirt rather Adam had to exist for her to be made. Man came first then woman. Neither came as superior to either, but she came as the period to God's creation. All things were in place prior to her arrival. Hence, Satan's attempt was to upset the perfect order of God by telling 'ishsah' she "*will not die*" in order to despoil the crowning glory of God's creation. Satan did this by opening her eyes to the choices of "good and evil." These are the same reasons Satan went after Jesus on the mountain of temptation, to entice Jesus while He was suffering His weakest moments in the desert. Satan's attempt was to despoil the kingdom of God through Jesus. Just as Satan went after the Glory of God who is Jesus, Satan went after the crown of the crowning glory of God's creation, woman. God crowned the glory of His creation 'ish' with the crown 'ishsah.' For to despoil the crown of the crown, is to destroy the crown.

But, in dealing with the story of the creation of man, there are three main points to consider. We might call them, 'the three step plan of God's creation' according to the creation account as recorded in Genesis 2.

First: The creation and forming of the earth. Second: From earth God made man. Third: From man God made woman.

Hence, the Bible's order for the development of humanity goes something like this. Without earth, there is no life. Man has no existence apart from mother earth and woman in turn who proceeded from man has no existence apart from man. Mankind's existence is perpetuated through woman and thus both become inextricably bound one to another, both finding their existence on mother earth, which in turn was created by God. Earth, God's footstool, can exist without life form, but life form, made out of the dust of the earth, cannot exist without earth. Therefore, if life is dependent on earth, then the continuance of life on earth is dependent on procreativity. What is synonymous with each is their interdependency. As life is dependent on

32

earth, procreativity is dependent on life. Such is representative of a creative God.

Yet, the need to procreate is not restricted to just the physical unions of human male/female sex organs. If that were the case, then rape along with recreational sex would also be included as a valid means of procreation. But, before the physical act takes place, the moral and spiritual standards of a union, as established by God, must first be fulfilled. The early Hebrews called it 'yada,' to know. In other words, yada, is not only a fusing of the genitals but it also includes a fusing of the minds and hearts of the couple. And as we have mentioned above, that union must meet the standards under the term, *"fit"* helper before made in the *"image of God"* has meaning.

Now without going too deeply into the ramifications of reproduction, it is understood, at least at this point, that man and woman are both physically and morally dependent upon each other. We are physically dependent upon each other for the continuation of the human race. To put it more succinctly, sex is not necessary for the survival of the individual but it is necessary for the survival of the human race. But it is the moral dependency we must look at more closely. Because of this moral dependency, humanity ranks far above the mating instincts in animals; for we must rise above the mechanics of instinctive mating and move into the realm of mate selection by means of reason, morality and spirituality based on standards set by God. These are the ingredients that set us apart from animals. These standards must be met so that man and woman can become equally yoked – for life. Here, womankind enters into the picture. Her role is one of awakening these values in man.

Yet, her role in man's spiritual awakening is not exclusively hers. Only with God, is she able to awaken these moral and spiritual values unique to the human family. *"It is not good that the man should be alone,"* was commanded by God not her. Hence, woman liberation and male domination has no place in God's standards set for humanity. Liberation and domination are kinship terms relative to the condition of sin. Neither of these events exists in the state of salvation nor did they exist before the fall. In either case, there is no sin to be liberated from because there is no domination of sin. It is with this understanding we enter into the mysteries of Genesis. For the writers of Genesis developed their views on male/female relationships from the interlocking relationship between man, woman, earth and God. Man is what he is because of what woman evokes in him. Woman is what she is because she is of the same substance of man. Both, were *"the image of God"* before sin. Since sin (Genesis 2), divine attributes in humanity changed. We are now from the dust.

Today, we are the products of sin, because today humanity is far removed from the male and female story as described in Genesis 1:27. We are today the humanity of Genesis 2ff. Jeremiah's description of humanity is *"The heart is deceitful above all things and desperately corrupt:"* (17:9a). While Isaiah claims, *"The whole head is sick..."* (1:5b). Therefore, since creation, just as man fell short of the glory so did woman. We were in the beginning created in God's image; but now, because of sin, we fall short of that initial image. Thus, as a consequence and as it stands today, whether or not we are or are not created (reproduced) in the image of God, is only one side of the argument. The other side, is whether or not all humanity is perpetuated in the image of God since the initial creation?

What must be considered; is being created in God's image and existing in sin, one in the same? Said another way, can one perpetuate in their sin and still be in the image of God? My response is no, for it does not stand to reason sociologically or theologically that one can perpetuate their existence in one's original state of innocence while living in a state of sin. Otherwise what purpose would salvation serve? If one is born innocent, one will not remain innocent whether or not we may or may not be born in God's image. What is at issue is our image after sin. In sin, we do not perpetuate our existence in the image of God, *"None is righteous, no, not one: ...since all have sinned and fall short of the glory of God"* (Rom.3ff). *"For the wages of sin is death..."* (Rom.6:23a).

Yet, we need to say something about the expression, *"in the image of God."* Diogenes Allen regards the fact that the advancement made in science will at the same time retreat the power of religion. He went on to claim that God is not a member of the universe He created. For if He were, He would be knowable in time to come with the advancements made in science. Religion would therefore become obsolete. But such a theory would be a contradiction to scripture that claims, *"who can know the mind of God...?"* Not only that, but the created is not a good source to positively identify with the image or likeness of the Creator. Dr. Allen addresses this by writing, *"...God's relation as Creator to the members of the universe is not the same as any of the relations that exist between its members."*[4] Simply put, we cannot know the image or likeness of God by studying His creation no more than we can determine the image of a man from a clay pot made by him. Hence, humanity and all its behavior problems are not a fair representation of the image of God.

To know humanity is not enough to know God. We come to know God through humanity only in so much as the Holy Spirit dwells in us. Therefore, in light of this, one cannot loosely use the expression that we are created, *"in the image of God"* without first qualifying that statement. Today, all of humanity has fallen far short of that initial image of God found in Genesis 1:27.

But we must not stop here. For Genesis 2ff unfolds before our eyes the origins of the coming of man into conscious being. This coming into conscious being was not of his own, but rather through the transforming power of a fit woman. We know the story as recorded in Genesis. This woman, a special woman, one *"fit"* for him (tailored exclusively for him), became that transforming ingredient in Adam. By the power of God working in her, she was able to awaken Adam into the realm of a conscious, mindful, warm, intelligent, spiritually alive, sensitive human being. For it was only after Adam had discovered his correspondent whom he named *"Eve,"* did he arrive at the true expression of himself. Only then could he use that magnificent gift of speech, in sentence form, when only moments before he could only mumble out names for animals. With this awakening experience, he was then able to fully express himself and marvel with conviviality, *"This at last is bone of my bones and flesh of my flesh..."*

Therefore, what both men and women must understand, is the important role she plays in his manhood awakening experience. Those needed ingredients of compassion and affection are significant requirements of his manhood. These ingredients lie dormant in man until woman comes along. This is the power that is active in a Godly woman of today. For with the help of the Lord, just as she is the

---

4 Allen, Diogenes, <u>Christian Belief in a Postmodern World</u>, p. 74.

vessel that ushers humanity into the world, she is also the source that is designed to awaken man into a conscious state. She has first opportunity of awakening in humanity those sensitive values of compassion and affection so germane to the moral and spiritual development of humankind. For, to whom else do men plant their seed?

We learn, furthermore, from Genesis that the Garden of Eden story begins as a 'non-role learning' love relationship which existed with the man and woman in their original sinless state; *"...the man and his wife were both naked, and were not ashamed."* *"This at last..."* cried Adam, *"is bone of my bone, flesh of my flesh"* which is to say, finally, I have discovered love. But after sin entered the union of Adam and Eve, their relationship veered off track. Sin now makes it necessary to build a relationship not on our love but rather on the premise of Divine love and having to learn the necessary duties and roles each must play in a marital relationship — in order for the union to survive. Their relationship had to be re-ordered on the foundations of duty and role.

We are commanded to love (Rom.13: 8-10). It is no longer within our person to love naturally or choose to love on our own. We can no longer love from the premise of our desires, how we feel (1John 4:7-12). We no longer have a choice to love God's way neither is it within our human nature to naturally love in accordance with God's standard. We must learn to love and or love by command. In either case love is a duty not a choice. We are commanded by God to perform this duty. Love is not human. God is love. Love does not originate with us, but with God!

To veer off track for a moment, we need to look at imperfect marriages existing in a sinful world.

Because sin entered humanity, marriage was instituted. Thus, marriage is based upon an established system of duties, rights, responsibilities, penalties, and an ordered structure. This is a must, in order to maintain a well ordered society! Marriage, therefore, serves a purpose in "...repressing irregular affections, to support social order..." Nowhere is marriage based solely on love apart from the performance of duty. A typical marriage vowed blends both love and duty: "...will you love and honor...forsaking all others, through sickness and in health..." Titus teaches that love is a training process along with duty, "...train the young women to love their husbands and children" (2:4), while being coupled with the performance of duty, "to be sensible, chaste, domestic, kind, and submissive to their husbands..." (5). In other words, duties performed give definition to love. See also Eph. 5:21ff.

In the O.T., marriage is a system of love, joined with rights and duties to perform: (Exodus 21:10 are rights; Genesis 29:31,32 and Proverbs 31:10-31 are duties to perform). What we see in Genesis 3:16-20 is the absence of the emotions of love in the Adam and Eve event. Love is not excluded in their relationship (although it is not mentioned), but duty, performance and penalty are strongly emphasized. Hence, what we see in marriages while existing in sin is the performance of duty; she shall, "...bring forth children... her desires shall be that of her husband's...by the sweat of his brow he shall work...he shall rule over her..." These are the foundations of a marriage in the state of sin, and love arises from these foundations.

Furthermore, from a Bible viewpoint, manhood cannot be

defined separate and apart from womanhood. In the Bible, the whole man is represented as man and woman being together in marriage. We read in Genesis, "It is not good that man should be alone;..." (2:18). Isaiah is very strong on this same point in that men and women are not viewed as separates. Isaiah writes when men are killed in war, "Seven women shall cling to one man..." forcing the women to resort to desperate measures in order to, "be called by their husband's name" to, "take away their disgrace" (3:25-41). In biblical times, not to be married was a disgrace. It left a numbing feeling of not belonging (See also Ez. 24:15-18).

But, before we proceed further in understanding manhood (to be completed in the institution of marriage), something should be said more specifically about black America's manhood. Black American men have had a unique experience in America which leaves issues and concerns unanswered pertinent to his developing manhood. Some experiences of black men in America have affected his concepts of manhood. For instance:

1. Blacks in general are <u>hypersensitive in racial matters</u>. What blacks in general must come to grips with is that the time and money spent on dealing with racial matters has a direct affect on their understanding of manhood in a racist society. We spend too much time defending who we are in a racist society and not enough time on discovering our maximum potentials.
2. <u>Self-hatred</u> is inseparable from hatred of others. Often the others in the black experience is identified as the opposite sex. We must come to grips with our sublime intolerance of our opposite sex. Neither sex must view the other as being their opponent.
3. <u>Black consciousness and black awareness</u> greatly

influence how blacks perceive themselves and their problems. Often the level of black awareness affects the level of the perception of black manhood. The less we know about our black history, the less we know about ourselves.

4. Finally, is the black culture in America <u>a dysfunctional culture</u>? Said another way, we know that the role of an oppressive society against people-of-color, is to create and maintain cultural deprivation, which in turn will produce predictable behavior in blacks. This predictable behavior works against us.

A further word about this predictable behavior is that it becomes too much of a subject of research and study of the black condition, in order to publish but not change. In other words, too many black programs to help blacks, hinge on documentation of the problem and less on contributions to the solutions.

But to come back on track, what must not go unnoticed, is the institution of marriage. The institution of marriage, in and of itself, is perfect. However, the marrying couples are not! What must be understood about marriage is it is defined in the imperative mode just as the Bible is written in the imperative mode. Marriage is therefore, not left to the marrying parties to define, biblically it is already defined!

From this foundation of a duty to perform and penalty as a result of sin, God proscribed boundary limitations so that Adam and Eve, while in the state of sin would not overshoot these boundaries and thereby risk losing their salvation. Both are thus commanded by God to play out their roles as husband and wife within the limits of His well-defined boundaries. ...To the woman, her well-defined boundaries are, "*...your desire shall be for your husband and he shall rule over you.*" Some would argue that this passage "your desire" is extended to all women, both single and married, in that she has little to no desire for sexual pleasure but rather for sexual purpose. However, this is an imperative by God commanding that she never make decisions independent of her husband and that her commitment to him is now an extension of his desires. Not only that, but being that she sinned against her husband, her commitment is to him. Said in another way, her desires and interests are to his desires and interests, as she is to him a companion (Proverbs 31:10-31). In other words, her desires and interests are not separate and apart from his consideration. Hence, her desires and interests must work in harmony with the total relationship and never at a disharmony. In a sense, her desire for God is greatly lessened by the increased desire she has for her husband.

For example, if she wants to work as a traveling sales lady and if being a traveling sales lady is proven to generate disharmony in the relationship, then no matter how strong her desire may be to practice her profession, she cannot practice it in that relationship. The marriage is superior to her personal desires. However, if she insists, then for that relationship she is not a "*fit*" helper. Thus, built into her "*fitness*" is not only the blessing of the "*image of God,*" but also the penalty of generating disharmony in the relationship should she fall short of that fitness which is the blessings of the image of God. Thus, the penalty for her submission (or desire for her husband), acts not only as her punishment but also as her blessing. Her punishment is that she has lost her freedom of unlimited boundaries to be and to do and must live out her days within the confinement of God's proscribed boundaries. For to live totally free in sin while a sinner, is to be totally lost in sin. Her blessing is that her doing and being, while having an increased desire for her husband, are restricted, so that she will not lose her soul. These restrictions, therefore, have nothing to do with male domination, but rather, sin domination. It is sin that wants to dominate her life (Gen.3:1-5), not man.

To the man "...*in toil you shall eat...all the days of your life...in the sweat of your face you shall eat...till you...*(die)." This is also an imperative by God so that the man will face up to and perform his responsibilities, and if necessary, above and beyond the call of normalcy. He must work; be there a reward or not, no excuses accepted. "*If any one will not work, let him not eat*" *(2Thess.3:10b)*. His role is thus proscribed within the parameter of these boundaries. As said in the words of Frederick Douglas, "...we may not get all we pay for but one thing for sure, we will pay for all we get." Hence, to the man, not only is God's breath of life a blessing to him but it is also the penalty he must pay should he sin; "*O Lord, thou hast searched me and known me!...Whither shall I go from thy Spirit? Or whither shall I flee from thy presence?*" *(Ps.139)*. In other words, man finds his blessings in obeying God, not fleeing from God. But the penalty he must pay, "...*all the days of (his) life...*" is that he will reap the consequences of his own sinful behaviors along with doing hard labor to earn an honest living. And God will not intervene to rescue him all the time. Man sinned against God and is now committed to work the earth. Once he was the caretaker of it. Now, the earth resists his care, "*thorns and thistles it shall bring forth to you...*" Hence, these two imperatives of God launched against man and woman, duty to perform and the accompanying penalty of sin to overcome, becomes the modus operandi of any relationship. Both duty and penalty comes built into every relationship.

Now, the one factor that makes the difference between the non-role love relationship (Gen.1: account of creation), and the need for learning the duties and roles in a relationship as just discussed, is sin. What must be understood is the built-in consequences just in knowing sin. One of these consequences is sin presents a different angle-of-view on a subject. What was once unashamed, *"[they] were both naked and were not ashamed"* is now made to be shamed, *"...the eyes of both were opened and they knew that they were naked."* Furthermore, sin removes boundaries to the imagination or actions of the sinner. But because of sin, the boundaries for which God sets for us is key to our salvation.

However, relationships of today are founded in the state of sin. For relationships, between male/female, rest on the foundation of mate expectation. (We have covered that above). In other words, we have already fixed in our minds the role we expect of our mates which because of the sin in both, is not the role mandated by God in Genesis. What happens in these types of relationships are that all our energy is burned up in castigating our mates for not having lived up to our expectations. If our expectations had been rooted in the sinless environment of the Garden of Eden love affair, before Satan entered the picture, then our expectations would be valid because they would be faultless. But this is not the case. Today, our relationships must withstand reality testing because we live in a faulty and sinful world. Therefore, what really happens is we begin with faulty expectations and move toward disappointment. Little is done in the way of learning the real duties and roles in a marriage <u>within the boundaries as proscribed by God</u>. But, in order to keep love alive in the marriage, both must subscribe to the mandate of God. For too small an emphasis is placed on the realities of married life. Furthermore, today imperfect relationships exist in an imperfect world. And because of sin, unions must be established on the foundations of love not exclusive of duty and role requirements. The duty and role requirements of a union are set by God. This standard of God for a sanctified union, as discussed above, becomes the modus operandi of the relationship. For since the fall, couples must now learn this modus operandi of marriage in order to keep love alive and the marriage sanctified.

Thus, in a marriage we must learn well this divine standard. The details of the modus operandi are played out within the proscribed boundaries established by God, as discussed in Genesis 3:16-19. However, should either or both of the couples still insist on their individual expectations being fulfilled, then both or either must also consider the flip side of their expectations. The flip side, simply put, is this; give back the same expectations you demanded from the other. But, whatever be the case, one thing is for sure love can no longer be non-role
identifiable as in the days of innocence before the fall. Love must find merit in clear-cut duties and roles in the union, in order for the union to perpetuate in love. Hence, in order to preserve the union, the modus operandi must be invoked, based on the standards established by God, because marriage is God created, not man made: "Then God said, it is not good that the man should be alone; I will make him a helper fit for him...from the man He made into a woman and brought her to the man" (Gen.2:18,22b).

The final mystery we learn from Genesis still springs from

the theme of male/female unification. This unification must exist in order to complete the fullness of manhood. For if the nature of God is one of unification, i.e., "The Father and I are One," The Father, The Son, The Holy Spirit; "Let us make man in our image, after our likeness;" all these being statements of solidarity, then God passed on to us His nature of solidarity. God is therefore, the God of unity and harmony. Because of this, man and woman in God, are locked into the bonds of mutuality. Simply put, she cannot ever be fully what she ought to be while single, no more than he can be fully what he ought to be without her.

Whatever they can fully be while single, comes to completion only when they are united. She can be a woman, singularly, but united, her womanhood comes to completion in wife hood and motherhood. He also can be a man singularly, but united to her as husband and father, his manhood comes to completion. She can make decisions singularly, but they will not carry the strength of a union. He can work to achieve a goal singularly, but his work would not be inspired by a union, neither would his labor fulfill a need in a union, nor will he discover a purpose for his labor beyond self-gratification nor will his labor find place and purpose in a union.

Hence, what must be realized is that the value of marriage is not measured in the doubling of resources, comfort in securities, or the moral thing to do.
Rather, what happens is when unions are formed in God, wholeness is brought to the union. A spirit of harmony pervades throughout the union. This spirit of harmony, as established by the standards of God, benefits and interfaces with all humanity. Nothing makes a man or woman more whole and socially accepted universally, than that of the

title of Mr. & Mrs. [wholeness-in-spirit, united in the Lord]. Hence, manhood entails a sense of wholeness united with his helper *"fit"* for him as established by God's standard. And if it is the standard of God, then man's wholeness finds completeness in his, *"helper fit for him."*

Therefore, the message is a message of unification for manhood and his wife according to the standards set by God. Men arrive in their manhood in so much as they include in their lives the full measure of the human ingredients given to them by God.

In summation, I must again stress the importance of a *"fit"* helper. Needless to say, this means a fit wife. But the whole business of the "fitness" concept has nothing to do with the quality or non-quality of the life of a person when they marry. Rather the secret of this "fitness" idea rests in the mind of God, as we have discussed. The wife was a *"fit"* helper of one kind before sin, and a *"fit"* helper of another kind, after sin. Before sin she was a *"fit"* helper without restrictions and after sin she is a *"fit"* helper within the clearly defined boundaries set by God. The details of each marriage must be worked out within the parameter of the modus operandi. Thus, the Bible dictum, "be ye not unequally yoked" has roots that penetrates to the core of one's bottom line character, married or single. "Unequally yoked" carries a much broader meaning than what meets the eye of immediate understanding. Put more succinctly, "For the unbelieving husband is consecrated through his wife and the unbelieving wife is consecrated through her husband" (1Cor.7:14), is not a statement of being equally yoked, spiritually or otherwise. Thus, a broader understanding of what it means to be "unequally yoked" must be considered.

What must be considered by anyone contemplating marriage is, how deeply seated in the character of the marrying couples are the common characteristics which make for a foundation to build on, in order to make any unequally yoked couple become yoked equally. In other words, if we penetrate into one's bottom line character, will we discover anything common to both as a starting point to build an equally yoked relationship? Not only that, but while living in a world of sin (where inequality is the norm), are partners in marriage willing to abide by clearly defined and pre-established limitations and boundaries and do they have the mental maturity and capabilities to do so? Said another way, while living in a world of sin, in order to be equally yoked, couples must have the emotional and intellectual maturity to abide by the clear-cut rules and requirements of marriage as proscribed by God. Thus, the bottom line character of both must bottom out at this point. It is within these clearly defined limitations and boundaries that couples must live out their lives in marriage. And all the things that couples do within these fixed boundaries become for that marriage the modus operandi. Yet, to clearly understand how the business of being equally yoked can exist in a sinful world of inequality, is to know and understand first the differences between marrying groups of people.

For instance; the first marrying group consists of two persons bad for each other. The next marrying group is one person that is bad for the other. The third marrying group is two good people marrying each other and the final group is two people that are good for each other in marriage. All of the marrying groups are faced with consequences, however, the final marrying group is the group for which the two find a foundation to become equally yoked. They are the ones who have the capacity to learn to live within the established boundaries set by God. Thus, from this relationship rises the universal standard of acceptable manhood; and, as for that matter, also, womanhood. For one 'hood' cannot be without the other. Such can be understood in the relationships between Sarah and Abraham, Elkanah and Hannah, Elizabeth and Zechariah and Joseph and Mary. Maybe the whole idea of manhood, womanhood and neighborhood is conveyed in these lyrics:

Join hands then, brother of the faith,
Whatever our differences may be;
For he who serves my Father as one,
Is surely kin to me.

November 13, 1977

Chapter Three

IT'S TIME TO WAKE-UP

(Variation of: John's Gospel: A Message of Liberation for the Black Church, [1978]) John 3:3-7; 4:13-15,28,29; 11:25,40-44; Romans 13:11-14

Today I believe the black church is being confronted with the monumental task of making a change. Not a regular change, but a cataclysmic change. This change must come about, in order to deal more effectively with the rapidly changing morals of black America. There is a *new wave of immorality* sweeping America for which our black communities are caught-up in. This *new wave of immorality* undergirds the current problems we already have. Blacks are already overloaded with undue stress, defensive behaviors and a host of insecurities. Thus, this *new wave of immorality*, only adds chaos to stress.

Today we witness more and more mindless crimes being committed by blacks than ever before; relationships between blacks are very loosely knit. It does not take much to kill a relationship. There is a level of self-willed ignorance raging among blacks today, unmatched in our historical record since we landed here in 1619. The state of Oklahoma, alone, sadly reports that there are "10 times as many black men in its prisons than are attending their colleges and universities." ...not counting, "...those that are in city and county jails."[1]

Self-serving greed, blind lust and no God consciousness, is almost a way of life. Today, more than ever before, I meet more and more blacks who have never set foot in a church.

---

1 <u>Setting A National Agenda For African-American Males</u>, a report by: The National Black Caucus of State Legislators held in Tulsa, OK, (April 15-17, 1993).

This worse case scenario is not only widespread, but is growing.

Thus, the black church can no longer stand by and view with indifference, these sins plaguing our communities. As in the past, the black church today must step forward to become more involved in the lives of blacks. We must take the lead in reversing the direction of these *sins which defect our personalities*, and do this with all deliberate speed. The problem is urgent because our black communities have already been for some time traveling at high speed, down the road of destruction into the abyss of nonexistence.

But today, and because of the nature of this *new wave of immorality*, we can no longer afford the luxury of the conservative approach. The current substandard moral, spiritual, and economic conditions of the larger black community dictates immediate action. And because of this, <u>it is time to wake-up</u>!

<u>It is time to wake-up because</u>...
I remember a time when the church doors were open all night long for prayer vigils, but we can't do that anymore...
I remember a time when we didn't mind coming back to evening and night service, when night service would begin, not end at 8 P.M., following BYPU. We would lift high our voices and sing; *"Now the day is over, night is drawing nigh, shadows of the evening, steal across the sky;"* but we can't do that anymore...
I remember a time when we could leave our coats and personal belongings on the coat racks in the church, and they would be there when we returned; but we can't do that anymore...
Not only that, but we must now lock up the house of God

with steel security bars and sophisticate burglary alarm systems so as the unsaved as well as the saved cannot steal from the house of the Lord. And because times have radically changed, the response of the black church must be radical, it must be cataclysmic...For it's time to wake-up! We can no longer afford to slumber in the luxury of having church on Sunday for the saved, while avoiding weekday encounters with those who are not saved: Having waited too long already to still the onrushing tide of our community problems and concerns...Having waited too long, in addressing the lack of spiritual maturity among the saved in the church, the black church is now faced with the harsh realities of having to face today's sins, not only in the streets, but also in the church... Because if the church refuses to go into the community, the community has no qualms in coming into the church. It's time to wake-up!

For example, in the communities, crimes are no longer crimes of passion but crimes of senselessness. Our nation's Capitol is raging almost out of control with senseless crimes in the homes and streets. There's talk now at the law enforcement level, as to whether or not to recruit assistance from the National Guards to assist in the fight against crime in the nation's Capitol.

Just the other day, a black man shot and killed a black police officer because he was irate at being kicked out of a local bar for unruly behavior... but this is not just one isolated incident... we are struck with many problems... both criminal and social. Where black on black crime is basically annihilating black men, it would appear that the social disease of AIDS is doing the same to black women.

The most current report as of June, 1996, from the Center on Disease Control, shows the AIDS crises in Ohio and the nation among black women is astounding. The report goes on to say that in a period of four years from 1992-1996, the cases in Ohio diagnosed with AIDS among women only, rose from 60 to 136. The report continues, "more than half the women with AIDS in the state are black." The national picture is even more dismal: Of 78,654 reported cases of AIDS in women only in the U.S., 58,991 are women of color. That means four out of five cases of known AIDS patients, are women of color. Somehow or other we are not getting the message.

But we also have problems with/in the church! In, now: With, later. We have problems in the church because what we discover is the behaviors that should have been addressed at the community, school or home level, must now be addressed in the church. But because the black church has delayed too long, in stilling the on rushing tide of black community immorality and ignorance, many bad behaviors have now seeped over into our churches. We find now that the black church, is faced with correcting behaviors that should have been corrected at the community or home level before they reached the church. Black churches today spend too much time, money and energy, replacing or guarding against property being stolen, damaged, or misused by persons with disrespectful or bad behaviors, who are both members and non-members of the church.

I've visited many black churches whereby all one has to do in order to measure the barometer of how genuinely one really respects their church and one another, is to look in one of the most inconspicuous places; the ladies' and men's restrooms. Restrooms tell us an awful lot about the people who belong to that establishment. Finally, there are congregations full of partiality love. In other words, we love some, but not others.

Thus in the process of the black church waking-up, not only must it wake-up to the external ills in the community, but it must also awaken to the internal will of God. But the wake-up must be complete. It must be complete in that not only is it time to just wake-up; but in the words of Romans 13:11, "it is <u>full time now</u>… to wake-up."

Yet, I need not stand here this morning and regurgitate vital statistics on the spiritual, social, moral, or economic conditions of blacks in America. All one needs to do is to look at the news to discover the bad news. *We have come a long ways baby! But! we've got a long ways to go and a short time to get there.* We are plagued with radical deficiencies in every area of our existing in America. From the political halls of justice to the entertainment capital of the world, we are faced both with quantitative and qualitative deficiencies. Deficiencies, for which I have come to believe, contribute to the reasons as to why our communities go so lacking.

For instance; on the political scene, our faces and voices are not seen or heard in proportion to the needs of the vast suffering black population. We are not seen or heard at all on the presidential or at the state governorship level, and seldom on the house and congressional levels.

As far as the Supreme Court goes, every now and then we find strength in a T. Marshall, just to keep the record straight for the cause of equal justice, or we will find alienation in a Clarence Thomas, as a reminder of what the record is, in that we've yet a long ways to go in order, to get the record straight.

On the Hollywood screen, we portray some of the most vulgar and often the most unrelated, demeaning and meaningless acting roles imaginable. Roles that give little to no attention to the harmonious meaning of relationships between black men and black women. Roles that set us at a disharmonizing distance. Roles played that are designed to keep us thinking unrealistically about ourselves and about those things we ought to be thinking realistically about. Too often we are cast into roles as being: Black male bashers, pimps, drug pushers and committing senseless crimes against our own. *FURTHERMORE AND TOO OFTEN WE ARE CAST AS BEING:* Too *super black,* whereby we are per-chance doing all the shooting of white men rather than getting shot by them; *Too vulgar,* where everybody's name is m.f., and the solution to every problem is s.o.b., and the only successful business is drug pushing and pimping black women; *Too middle-class,* whereas black men are featured as heads of households in a Dagwood Bumstead fashion. In other words, he's there to complete the image of a middle-class family, but is portrayed as a clumsy bumbling retard, having to always apologizing to his wife for some dumb mistake he made. In turn, this leaves her, to play the role of the real brain of the family, who always appears to be the super black woman who stays cool, calm and together, or; *Too Alice-in-wonderland like,* i.e., they lived happily ever after. Well! black folk don't live happily ever after; nobody! lives happily ever after. They may live out happy moments every now and then, but not every moment is happy ever after. We are too suspicious, distrustful, jealous and resentful towards one another to live happily ever after with anybody. I know this to be true because if we did not possess any of these negative characteristics, our divorce rate would not be five out of ten plus. Black on black crime and AIDS would not be numbered among the leading cause of death for blacks. And, with a Gross National Income of $400 plus billion for blacks, we would not be at the bottom rung of the economic latter while being the largest minority group in America and living in the richest nation in the world for the longest period of time of any minority group, not native to this country! Happiness does not create these results.

Little do we suspect that the models set before us through the electronic airways, is by design, programming our minds to think and believe that 'this is how things really are.' It closes our eyes to realities. But the most damaging of all is that our heroes come from the world of entertainment and not from the history books of reality. We would much rather recreate than educate, delight rather than enlighten.

From the halls of educational fame to the socioeconomic situations of our communities, if we would only open our eyes to the community around us, and close them to the TV world of fantasy and shame, we would see a disproportionate amount of glaring economic deficiencies and despairing living conditions among blacks. For every city in America, has it's own black ghettoes, composed of both black men and women. Blacks are 32.8 million strong and $400 plus billion rich, yet blacks still occupy the bottom rung of the economic ladder, heading downward. You see, not only do we not know how to live together happily, but also, we have not yet learned how to distribute our wealth among ourselves in order to get some happiness.

But don't read me wrong.
Many attempts have been made to distribute the black wealth of the nation among our own, but for the most part,

they were made in vain. We have not yet learned the art of enterprising, corporate unity and the consolidation of power. But the sad part of it all is that in every black economic report I read the trend for positive economic change for the black condition is dim. One report concluded, "Black Americans... remain the poorest group in America." At best according to another report blacks might realize a "modest improvement." This is a very sad commentary; for when we look at our current economic trend, black economic spending habits looks like this: Blacks' gross income for 1996 was over $400 billion. That's a lot of money. But blacks spent $500 billion. The point to be made is that blacks have questionable spending behaviors. What must therefore be questioned, is our spending habits keeping us at the lower end of the economic ladder? Blacks end up either owing more than they make, or paying out all they earn. Blacks are not educated in the schools of production but rather raised in the environments of consumption. Blacks' spending habits along with their lack of interest in networking, corporate investments, commercial enterprising and business corporations need to be questioned.

In other words; what does the picture of black spending priorities and habits look like, and does this picture tell something of the whys of their conditions?
In 1996 blacks spent:
$93 billion + in housing/furniture...
$44 billion in food...
$20 billion in clothing...
$11 billion in health care products...including vitamins pills...
$11 billion in new cars...
$9.5 billion on the telephones...
$6 billion on entertainment and travel...

$4.5 billion in personal care products...perfumes, ties, shoes, lipsticks, hairdos, jewelry...
$4 billion on personal computers and electronics...
$3 billion on education...

You see, if we take a look at the money blacks make and their spending behavior, and compare this with their attitudes towards education, I think one can see why, as a community, blacks stay at the subsistence or poverty level all the time. *To say it another way, there was $294 billion that past through the hands of black people last year that went elsewhere other than on education.* There can be no mistake made about why blacks cannot escape the jaws of poverty and ignorance with that great amount of money in the hands of a people that place such little interest on education. The black Gross National Income is not misappropriated but rather it is disproportionate. Blacks got the money but they do not know what to do with it. One learns from these figures, that a consistent pattern of spending is revealed. Black people consistently do not change their spending habits.

Our black schools must beg for money to stay open, black hospitals are practically non-existing and as we speak blacks have little to nothing in the way of a defense program that will prove effective enough to stop the onslaught of the mass annihilation of black people. And this mass annihilation is taking place by means of: Drugs, black crime on crime, ignorance, prison, [blacks are 12.6% of the U. S. population but make up about 50% of the prison population]. To give you an idea of what this looks like in numbers, in 1994 there were about 1 million men and women in prison. About one-half of these are black. Blacks lack in basic educational skills, in order to exist in this high-tech society, they have low political clout, [there is only about 50 black people in Washington to speak for about 33 million black Americans].

Furthermore, we have a very poor social and crises intervention system that will address a black family in distress, as opposed to one of the spouses running downtown to the court to get a divorce just because they don't have to take that s.... You see, blacks have no defense against those things that are destroying them right now.

But the irony of it all is that the black church of historical past was actively visible in addressing the abject conditions existing in black communities. For instance: It served as a place that united a scattered suffering mass of slaves. It legislated patterns of behavior on how the slave should act in the face of overpowering odds so that the slave would not be killed. It was the support of the floundering black family and often it was the mother and father to homeless and parentless children. It was the authority and father figure in the absence of a father in the home. It was the mutual aid society to bury the dead, care for the sick and poor. It was an institution of education for blacks. It was a political arena for blacks that did not know what and who to vote for. *But what about today???* Well, today, as with yesteryear, the black church must be our advocate. There is hope, but the church is a sleeping giant that must be awaken! And it must be awaken with new resolve.

Dr. Martin Luther King, 30 years ago, rung the alarm clock in the ears of the sleeping giant when he said, "The church must become increasingly active in social action outside its doors… it must exert its influence in the area of economic justice. As guardian of the moral and spiritual life of the community the church cannot look with indifference upon these glaring evils."

And Malcolm X shook the sleeping giant when he said...
"Jesus himself was ready to turn the synagogue inside out and upside down when things weren't going right. "In fact," he went on, "in the book of Revelations,... Jesus [is] sitting on a horse with a sword in his hand, getting ready to go into action."

So, today, the work of the black church is cut out. For it must become the work of liberation. No longer can the black church look with indifference upon the glaring evils in our communities and do nothing. The black church must get ready to go into action. And we must take our clue for action from the gospels. For where Dr. King rung the alarm clock and Malcolm X shook the sleeping giant, Jesus Christ in Luke's gospel was there to wake-up the giant when he said: "The spirit of the Lord is upon me, because He has anointed me to preach the Gospel to the poor, proclaim release to the captives, give sight to the blind, to set at liberty those who are oppressed..." (Luke 4:18).

Black people today are not physiologically enslaved but rather psychologically enslaved. It ain't all whitey's fault today! Blacky shares in the largest portion of our psychological enslavement. And we need to be awakened from it. Yes! Maybe even a rude awakening.

Back during the early part of this month, President Clinton's address to the nation was a call to action out of an urgent need. He said that the..."National Educational Standard for what every student should know, ought be raised..." and the educational system "must have the best teachers available." One of the reasons, he stated, for this change was that "40% of 8 year olds, cannot read."

The black church can take a clue from the President's address in that, we need to raise our church standards of practicing Christianity. You see I am a firm believer that if the home is not right, then the church can not be right. But not only do we need to get the home right, but we also need to engage in community church networking. We need to do this by pooling our church resources to join in the fight against poverty, ignorance, crime and illiteracy, raging in our communities. And we need to begin at a point that is reachable for the black church and teachable to it's members... If we cannot begin with the political system, *where not only would we need to be in control of the Government, but also in control of its military might...* then we can start with the institution of education; *though it is a giant for which today black folks are going to need more than a David's stone to throw. We do have the money and we are teachable...* We could also start with the workforce; although we do not own the job markets, but with a change of priorities, it would be a good place to start.

I came across an interesting observation recently concerning the black job condition and it reported that, "Blacks, unlike other groups, have traditionally stressed social acceptance by whites, rather than making money [for enterprising] and the development of business enterprise." In other words, because we spend much time, energy and money on countering racism, supporting affirmative action programs, equal employment opportunities and etc., there is not much money, time and energy left to build businesses, schools and neighborhoods. This report went on to say that there is not "one black owned commercial bank" in the country. Privately owned but not a single commercial banking enterprise. You see, we could place more focus on our own resources and less on blaming whitey and racism.

But I wonder, can the black church even on the local scene, make a dent in the economic conditions of our people? Here in our own city, with over 227 listed black owned churches, not counting the unlisted ones, why can't we have a positive impact on the economic conditions of our black community... that's a good place to start! And I believe the gospel of John gives us a clue as to how we can get started. It is a clue rooted in a sudden and cataclysmic break with old behaviors. It is a clue rooted in Jesus' teachings, for we are challenged by Jesus to use all our mental, emotional and physical energies to deny [absolutely] any system which will keep us in poverty and shame. In other words, the teachings of Jesus are not only liberating, but also cataclysmic. They jar the inner being of our existence, in other words, "you must be born again" is more than a notion. We are never the same when confronted with the Master's teachings. We become transformed, we witness a new beginning and we are resurrected into a new life.

But the problem we have with the black church of today, is that it has failed to transform the larger black community. It has failed to give new beginnings to the welfare, homeless, poverty-stricken and crime-ridden communities of today. It has failed to resurrect from ashes, the crime-ridden black ghettos of America.

YET, THERE IS HOPE!
In the gospel of St. John, John records three personalities which symbolizes three church models of approaches to aid in the solutions to our community problems:

1. In the story of Jesus and Nicodemus, the church is an agent of community TRANSFORMATION!
2. In the story of Jesus and the Samaritan woman, the

church is an agent of community, NEW BEGINNINGS!

3. In the story of Jesus and Lazarus, the church is an agent of community RESURRECTION!

FIRST, THE GOSPEL OF THE BLACK CHURCH TO THE COMMUNITY MUST BE A GOSPEL OF TRANSFORMATION. WE MUST TRANSFORM OUR COMMUNITIES THROUGH EDUCATION AND THE GOSPEL OF JESUS CHRIST.

We remember the story of Jesus and Nicodemus, how Nicodemus came to Jesus by night to question The Master about this business of being re-born.

First, he was not a dumb man neither was he a heathen. He was a man of great learning, very religious, and head of the council of Pharisees. Jesus Himself even had to acknowledge Nicodemus' academic astuteness. For Jesus was astounded over the fact that Nicodemus could not understand the differences between flesh and spirit in spite of his great scholarship, "Are you a teacher of Israel and you do not understand these things?"

What we must realize is that Nicodemus had everything going for him. He had position, a daily living routine, public recognition and religion. But, in spite of it all, there was a defect in his central personality. And during this long conversation with Jesus, Nicodemus got absolutely nowhere with the Master, because of this defect. You see folk can go to church every Sunday, have a good job and income, good home, friends, family... and still *get nowhere with Jesus*. One does not have to be on the bottle, drugs, commit mindless crimes, in order to be *nowhere with the Lord*. You can have everything and be in church every

Sunday and still be *nowhere with the Lord.* For if Jesus is not the *center of your personality, then there can be no transformation in order to <u>get</u> anywhere <u>with</u> Jesus.* In other words, the Kingdom of God does not come by means of our mortal achievement, but by means of a transforming experience, "You must be born from above."

So it is with the black church. The church can get nowhere with the community, just by being in the community. For just as the transforming experience for the individual is Jesus at the center of their personality, the black church must become the *center of the personality* of the black community so that it may become the *transforming experience* for the black community. This means that collectively, the black church must not only be the voice of hope to the larger black community, but it must also be a voice of consciousness to the wealthy and knowledgeable black community leaders. We must say to them in the midst of this raging *new wave of immorality*, that somehow and for some reason $294 billion dollars did not reach the ignorant, the poverty stricken, the black ghettos, black youth gangs, drug ridden communities, black on black crime, research for the cure of AIDS, black schools and colleges begging for monies... There is a defect in the central core of the personality of the community and the church needs to be there to make it right. Our communities must be transformed—<u>They must be born again</u>, and the church must be the agent of community transformation. Someone wrote, Get Right Church and Let's Move On...

SECONDLY, THE GOSPEL OF THE BLACK CHURCH MUST OFFER <u>NEW BEGINNINGS</u> FOR OUR PEOPLE. THE CHURCH MUST GUIDE THE COMMUNITY TOWARDS A NEW BEGINNING. THE CHURCH MUST BE THE HEADLIGHTS OF THE COMMUNITY

LEADING IT <u>OUT</u> OF THE DARKNESS <u>OF</u> THE
GHETTOS, AND NOT THE TAILLIGHTS, GOING
ALONG WITH THE FLOW <u>OF</u> THE COMMUNITY
WHILE <u>IN</u> THE GHETTOS.

Again, we remember the story of Jesus and the Samaritan
woman. By the time Jesus met this black (Samaritan)
woman, segregation between Jews and Samaritans had
lasted more than 400 years. Hence, she belonged to a class
of people that were looked down on. Having lived with
five husbands in the past, now shacking with a sixth man,
with her eye on Jesus as number seven, she was not by any
standard considered to be a respectable woman and Jesus
refused to feed her ego. Not only that, but she was also a
woman of religion. She worshipped something, even if she
didn't know what she was worshipping - as Jesus puts it.
Here was a woman as with Nicodemus, without meaning
to her living. She's looking for somebody to love. She has
a daily routine of hauling water, looking for new lovers and
playing religion. Yet, her life was unfulfilled. This woman
needed a life. She needed a *new beginning*. And her new
beginning came when Jesus became the center of her
personality. Her new beginning started at the well. The
water, she asked the Master, "which wells up to eternal
life" let me drink it. Jesus' reply, "I who speak to you am
the Christ." These were the words that opened the door to
her *new beginning*. No longer was she interested in her
daily routine of hauling water, no longer was she interested
in her lovers or religion... Because her *new beginning* was
standing right in front of her, "Come see a man who told
me all that I ever did..." And the question she proposed,
"Can this be the Christ?" became for her from that day
forward, *new life*!

So it is with the black church. It must be that *living water* in a community of not only black dead men walking, but also for black game-playing women talking. It must be for the hopeless, *a word of encouragement* and for the lost, *new beginning*. For the unbended knee in the community, the church must be a *prayer;* unread book, *a Bible;* unattended service, *an evangelist;* unrealized Cross of Jesus, *the hope of salvation;* uncompassionate heart, *love;* and for the lost soul, *Amazing Grace.*

If the church expects to answer "when the roll is called up yonder," it should be present in the community while the roll is being called down here.

FINALLY, THE GOSPEL OF THE BLACK CHURCH MUST OFFER HOPE WHEN ALL HOPE IS LOST. IT MUST BE THE HOPE OF THE <u>RESURRECTION</u> FOR BLACK COMMUNITIES LOST IN A HOPELESS CYCLE OF PERPETUAL GENERATIONS OF POVERTY, DESPAIR, WELFARE, GANGS AND DRUG RIDDEN COMMUNITIES.

The story of Lazarus is a story of a man resurrected by Jesus after death. It demonstrates that even when all is lost, Jesus can even reach beyond the boundaries of hopelessness and resurrect a soul into a new life. As dead Lazarus was raised unto new life from out of the stink of dead rotting flesh, new communities can emerge from out of the ashes of poverty, ignorance and despair.

The story of Lazarus is a story of complete separation from the impossible entanglement of the past. It is a story that liberates from even the most hopeless situations. For we learn even the most hopeless situations in the hands of Jesus, is not an impossible situation. There is an old Army slogan that goes like this; *"The difficult we do with ease, the impossible takes a little longer.*" But with Jesus, in the face of impossible odds, the answer is always the same. "Behold," writes Jeremiah, "I am the Lord the God of all flesh; is anything too hard for me?" (Jer.32:27).

Lazarus, whom Jesus loved, represents the lost victims in any society beyond human hope. Yet, when we read the story of Lazarus we discover four things about him that is not beyond the reach of God.

1. He was a "certain man" not just any person. Black people are special to God.
2. Who was "ill." Many of our communities are ill.
3. Whose name means "God helps." The Psalms tell us "God is our help and strength, a very present help in trouble." (46:1). We know how to call on the Lord...
4. He was from a village named Bethany, (house of poor).

Our communities are often poor without reason. But, God being our help, we have no need to be poor.

The story of Lazarus typifies a black community so downtrodden in poverty, drugs, gangs, crime, oppression, fear, ignorance and sickness, that the end result is the death of the community. But, as Jesus was the resurrection event for Lazarus, the black church is the resurrection event for the black community. For out from the black church, needs to flow a religion that can address the hopelessness of our communities.

Just the other day I watched a documentation on TV, pertaining to black gangs in several of our large cities in America. Gang members were being interviewed, ages 11-

18. Their testimonies were that killings in their communities were a way of life. With their nonchalant approach to killing, they testified, that if a rival gang member killed one of theirs, they would retaliate, "that's the way it is." One testified that there is not a single day that goes by whereby there isn't a drive-by, or killing every 20 minutes, every day.

One 15-year-old boy told his mother that he was just tired of gangbanging. A few moments later, a gunshot was heard in his bedroom. He had blown a hole in his head. <u>He was tired of the killing</u>. While the interviewer was filming this documentary, they caught on tape, a drive-by shooting. They showed the morgue and nothing but young black boys, were lined-up on slabs with toe tag identifications.

But thank God! Of all the social activities that tried to calm the raging tide of killing, one lone black church stepped out on faith and in less than one year, entered into a truce with rival gangs by planting 3,000 flags for each time a truce was made. This act alone cut the killing by 25%. But, what if all the black churches throughout America would come together? I believe that after all is said and done, when the church truly awakens, it will ultimately live out its true mandate captured in this song:

There's a church within us, O Lord,
There's a church within us, O Lord.
Not a building, but a soul, Not a portion, but a whole,
There's a church within us, O Lord.

There's potential within us, O Lord; Something's stirring
within us, O Lord. Something's straining to have birth,
To be visible on earth.

69

There's potential within us, O Lord.

There's some building to be done, O Lord, There's some
building to be done,
O Lord.
Not with steel, not with stone, But with lives which are
our own,
There's the church to be built, O Lord.

February 23, 1997

Chapter
Four

INSIGHTS INTO TITHES AND TITHING

Malachi 3: and Matthew 23:23-24

To maximize the importance of a single event over other events of equal importance in a common category is to minimize the importance of the other event(s) in the same category. The words of Jesus in Matthew 23:23 fit within the framework of this maxim.

Yet, we need to expound on this maxim in a way so as not to hint at or change the sayings and or meanings of our Lord on tithing in anyway. To do this, we need to look at the caustic remarks made by Jesus to the scribes and Pharisees. Jesus harshly ridiculed these scribes and Pharisees for placing maximum interest on tithing and none on the more "...weightier matters of the law, justice and mercy and faith." To Jesus, "It is these, you ought to have practiced without neglecting the others" (23). Hence in a nutshell, if one is going to tithe, then their interest in tithing should not be more important than the interest in the law of, "justice, mercy and faith" which is the more superior commandment of the law in any case.

What must be considered about tithing is, Jesus is neither objecting to nor commanding it. Rather, He is objecting to the near neurotic behavior and interest the scribes and Pharisees place on tithing over the "weightier matters" of the law. In other words, the "weightier matters...justice and mercy and faith," are being ignored by the scribes and Pharisees while tithes are being religiously and fanatically ritualized. The "weightier matters" (23) to which Jesus is referring, is imbedded in the "commandment in the law" 22:36-40; (also see Micah 6:8). This is what Jesus is referring to when He spoke, "these you ought to have done without neglecting the others" – "the others," are the tithing of dill, mint and cummin.

These herbs have their own level of significance in the use of healing and food seasoning, but they have nothing to do with practicing justice, mercy, and faith. However, what is important is the "commandment in the law" vis-à-vis "weightier matters," which is key to worshipping and gaining favor with God. But too often tithing (which is understood in terms of money) in the Bible* as well as in our churches of today, is used in a sublime way as an attempt to gain favor with God. For example, in Acts 8:20, Simon thought he could gain special favor from God by paying money. Peter corrected him by letting him know that "(his) heart is not right before God" (21). Peter let him know it is not the money that makes our hearts right before God, no matter what form or intent the giving may be, but rather it is a right heart before God (22).

Tithing, though not spoken of as being outlawed in the New Testament (N.T.) and the gospel of Jesus, is also not commanded by Jesus or by any other person or doctrine anywhere in the N.T. Tithing has no significant foothold in the gospel of Jesus. The gospel of Jesus is about salvation and "seek(ing)...first the kingdom of God and His righteousness..." (Matt.6:33). However, it is important to know that while the gospel is about the good news of Jesus and His message of salvation and the kingdom of God, it is equally important to know that Jesus is also the center of the gospel. For the gospel is Jesus. It is what He did and what He said. Thus, what Jesus did and what He said about tithing is Jesus! Also, what Jesus did not do and did not say about tithing is equally Jesus. His attitude towards

---

* Due to the frequent references to the Old and New Testaments of the Bible, I will often use O. T. and N. T. respectively in this paper, with a few exceptions, to show emphases.

tithing and what He had to say about it is the only divine source of authority we have to go on. Events or matters pertaining to tithing and both of Jesus' approaches to tithing are reflected in 23:23.

Furthermore, tithing is not mentioned by the writer of St. Mark, nor by Jesus in St. Mark. Mark, we must remember, is also the most pristine narrative of the other acclaimed gospels and is the only book in the Bible, which claims to be the gospel of Jesus. Hence, this silence on the issue of tithing in St. Mark is not by accident. Thus, tithing is not a subject germane to the gospels or unique to the events of the N.T. Rather, tithing is an evolutionary event, having beginning and ending in the Old Testament (O.T.).

Tithing was still in the process of evolving when it found its way into the advent of the N.T. and when it did, those who practiced tithing met with biting criticisms from Jesus. Furthermore, tithing found no place in the development of the N.T. primitive Christian church (Acts 2:43-47; 4:32-37; 5:1-11). What must be remembered is that the idea of tithing never caught hold in the N.T. church because the era for which tithing was rooted came out of the distinctive ideas of O.T. corporate community living. The distinctive idea of O.T. government is communal, not individually centered. Malachi 3:6-12, is a language, which addresses the community of the "children of Israel."

On the other hand, the N.T., is more rooted in a political system of privatization and the protection of the individual right of ownership of personal property. In Acts, as cited above, an attempt was made at O.T., community living, but failed in the face of the 5th chapter of Acts. What we see here is an early encroachment of the right to private and personal property ownership. The idea of O.T., communal living as implied in the scripture "...no one claimed private ownership of any possessions..." (4:32), was rejected in the face of the encroaching social order of the times as to the right of individual ownership of private property. An unholy bond developed between owner and property. This is implied in the Ananias and Sapphira story.

Hence, the resistance to tithing in the N.T. was the shift from O.T. community tithing responsibility to that of the individual's responsibility to tithe. The social order of the N.T. day was one of personal wages earned and the individual right to own personal property. Such an idea flew, in the face of the distinctive O.T. idea of communal tithes. For the right to personal property ownership in the N.T. implied that one not be fully detached from their personal property and money because they earned it. In a communal type society, no such thought of the right to private ownership was ever entertained. In other words, an unholy bond developed between wages earned and the wage earner, between owner and property. What, therefore, took the punch out of tithing in the N.T. era is this unholy bond between owner and property. The idea of private ownership tends to leave a lasting bond between personal and or private property and owner. Therefore, from a spiritual point of view, the unholy implication in private ownership is that one can never be fully detached from what they own, even if they give it to the church (See Mark 7:1-13 on Corban).

Private ownership was preferred over communal living, because in private ownership not only does property ownership give one status and power, but one could still, in part, profit from the part given away because one becomes bonded to their money and property. Peter pointed this out in (Acts 5:4). "While it remained unsold, did it not remain your own? And after it was sold, were not the proceeds at your disposal?" Also, Jesus was faced with the same issues of people bonding with their personal possessions. "No slave can serve two masters...You cannot serve God and wealth" (Luke 16:13, NRSV). The point to be made is tithing carried little to no spiritual strength in a private and personal ownership society because the tither was still attached to their tithe in some unholy way. For example: In Acts 8:18ff, Simon tried to buy the Holy Spirit with money. In other words, the thought is, give me something for my money. I am not going to just give my money away. In 5:1-4, Ananias and his wife schemed to continue to make money from their pretentious giving. In Luke 18:10ff, as with the Pharisees, some folk tithe and attach to their faithful activity of tithing the expectation of some favor or recognition in return. Somehow, the history of tithing does not act in favor of detaching us from our tithes. This is the unholy implication of bonding to wealth and tithing.

However, the issue on tithing reached its pinnacle in Matt. 23:23 when Jesus addressed it to the Jews. But what must be considered here is that Jesus' address on tithing was to the worshipping Jews in the temples, not Christians in the Christian church. Just as "all who sold and bought in the temple" (Matt. 21:12,13) was a Jewish issue and not a Christian issue, tithing was also a Jewish temple legalistic issue not intended to be a part of the coming age of grace and the church. Said another way, the keeping of tithing is only as good as the keeping of the whole law. Tithing was caught in the wave of a religious transitional blend of the old Jewish legal traditions of law and worship and the beginnings of the Christian era. However, what may be considered to be at issue and is common to both Judaism and Christianity is the medium of exchange for services and goods. We call it money. Money was and or is the most common and important factor in both religions, in spite of the fact that Jesus tried to rule out money in the new order of worship (see below).

However, if tithing is to be practiced, then it is not to be practiced to the exclusion of "justice and mercy and faith," the "weightier matters" and "the commandments of the law." Hence, the attitude of Jesus on tithing in Matt. 23:23 is one which demonstrates that to Him, tithing has no value or merit aside from the practice of the whole law.

Yet, the scribes and Pharisees totally missed this point of tithing. They argued the importance of only tithing while totally ignoring that tithing by itself is an insignificant part of the total picture of practicing "justice and mercy and faith." They tithed but did not practice "justice and mercy and faith." But as far as Jesus is concerned, to tithe and "neglect" at the same time "justice and mercy and faith" results in nothing more than producing "blind guides" thereby causing everyone to become spiritually blind, both tithers as well as the teachers of tithing (Matt.23:24). Alone, tithing serves no useful purpose. It has no rewards or favor with Jesus (23), neither does it have any salvation merits (24). Vischer has this to say:

"In the New Testament the payment of the tithe is of no significance. It is mentioned only occasionally and then as an element of Jewish legalistic piety. Jesus accuses the Pharisees of paying the tithe with absolute exactness and of overlooking the important elements of the law... Nowhere...does the New Testament demand that a yearly tithe is to be paid; neither Christ himself nor his disciples knew anything of such commandment. This silence is not accidental...; Christ questions whether we should have any

possessions at all...possessions have the character of an idol. They can become the object of a man's faith... It is, therefore, part of the fulfillment of the First Commandment that we completely free ourselves of all bondage to our possessions... It is for this reason [Jesus] sends his disciples out without any possessions at all: They are to preach the gospel in complete trust in God... It is clear that this viewpoint leaves no room for a Christian tithe..."[1]

Thus if Jesus' quote in Matt. 23:23 is viewed as a maxim, then it would probably read as follows: When one maximizes the requirements of tithing over the "weightier matters" of the law which is "justice and mercy and faith," they at the same time *minimize the maximum importance* of the spirituality in the things they "ought to have done ." The "weightier matters" are required by the Lord and the "commandment in the law." Therefore, tithing singularly finds no place of importance in the gospel of Jesus Christ. Tithing may even prove to be harmful to one's spiritual growth, for "Christ questioned whether we should have any possessions at all...possessions have the character of an idol," (Vischer).

INSIGHTS

First Insight:

THE ECONOMICS OF TITHING

Much religious language has been written on the subject of tithing and no doubt as long as the church exist or any type religious institution, more will be written 'til time shall be no more.' The authority for tithing, as assumed by most Christian church denominations, is rooted in Malachi 3ff.

---

1 Lukas Vischer, <u>Tithing in the Early Church</u>, p. 9-10.

However, a closer look at Malachi reveals a certain rationale for tithing often overlooked by the churches. For instance, we know that by the time Malachi was written, the second temple had been built, but the irony of this is that the people's hearts as well as the hearts of the priests were not in their worship. They had become sloppy in their worship to God. Malachi accused the Jewish community of dishonoring God by placing polluted food on the altar and sacrificing blind, lame, and sickly animals to God (1:13). They had no spirit for worship. What's more, it was the Gentiles who magnified God's name "...from the rising of the sun to its setting..." (11) whereas Israel, God's chosen, profaned God's name (12). Furthermore, the priests were not guarding the true Torah (2:1,2; see 10-12) and, *"To make matters worse, the people were complaining that serving God did not 'pay off,' as a matter of fact they even complained that 'Everyone who does evil is good in the sight of the Lord, and he delights in them. Where is the God of justice?' (2:17). "Why serve God if religion yields no tangible benefits?" (3:13-15). "Despite the vigor of Malachi's critique, the prophet himself does not measure up to the stature of his predecessors. He suggested that if the people would only present a tenth (tithe) of their income and stop 'robbing God' of what was due him, then Yahweh would pour out to them a great blessing, and Israel would be great among the nations (3:6-12)."*[2] However, the quote, "the prophet himself does not measure up to the stature of his predecessors" does not exclude Malachi himself in that "Yahweh's purpose, first of all, is to refine the priests, purifying them until they present 'right offerings' to Yahweh; and then his judgment will fall upon sorcerers, adulterers, false witnesses...(3:1-5)."[3] What needs to be considered from the above is that the

---

2 Bernhard W. Anderson, <u>Understanding the Old Testament (3rd Edition)</u>; (p.487).
3 Ibid.

issue of tithing is addressed to Israel, God's chosen people, not to the Gentiles.

Hence, Malachi [my messenger] is speaking the word of God to Israel because the word of God has become a burden (oracle) to Malachi (1:1) because of Israel's sloppy worshipping experiences. Malachi suggested that if the people would only present a tithe of their income and stop complaining then Yahweh would pour out to them a great blessing (3:10).

Hence, this certain rationale for tithing not only grew out of earlier conditions for tithing, (built into the law), but also tithing was a compensatory act of Israel ritualized by them in their worship, as a result of their sloppy worshipping habits. It was in hopes that by tithing, the act of tithing would compensate for their sloppy worship habits.

But to understand the impact of Malachi's burden is to understand that he has lived through a period of time for which the priests despised God and their solemn vocation as priests. Thus, Malachi dominates his thoughts with fidelity to the Lord's covenant and teachings (2:1-9); and charges that the priests are to stop robbing God by tithing profane offerings (1:12,13) while having no spirit for worship (3:14); and complaining and accusing God (2:17). Said another way, if one is going to tithe, do it the right way! It is not the tithe that counts, but the spirit in and of tithing. In other words, sloppy worship habits cancels out the true meaning of tithing. This is the same message being conveyed in Matt. 23:23,24; as well as in Mal. 1:11 where the integrity of the Gentiles' worship was preferred over Israel's profane acts of tithes (12).

However, tithing is a subject that needs reckoning. In the church, tithing needs reckoning in light of how it addresses both the economics and the spiritual ministry of the church. In other words, the church's financial obligations must be met as with any other secular institution. Moreover, the carrying out of the spiritual ministry of the church must also be sustained with money.

Yet, the paying of tithes for the above reasons is not, nor should it be understood or treated as a New Testament mandate or a prerequisite for salvation. Tithing should not be the focus of a religious tenant, a denominational mandate, or taught as being the index to one's salvation. Tithing should not be taught as a biblical principle for the expressed purpose of it being a prerequisite to one's salvation, or to be used against a practicing Christian in such ways as to making it become a spiritual stumbling block to their growth in Christianity. Alienating a convert from the main Christian stream and not fully accepting them into the Christian family until they pay their tithes, is a deliberate insult and an arrogant slap in the face of the author of John 3:16, as well as the gospel of Jesus Christ! What needs to be understood is, tithes should not be treated nor are they intended for anything other than what they were meant to be: Numbers 18:21, for services rendered; Amos 4:4,5, for celebrations; and Deuteronomy 14:28,29, for support of the needy. These are all tithes done in the right spirit.

Second Insight:

TITHING, THE WORD OF GOD AND THE WORD OF THE PROPHETS

What need to be considered are two arguments on tithing:

The first argument favors tithing as a Bible mandate falling under the aegis that the Bible is the whole word of God; therefore, tithing is also the word of God. The second argument favoring what is written or spoken about the word of God is the same.

The fault in this first argument also applies to Genesis 3:4,5. I doubt seriously that the lie Satan told to Eve in that story is the word of God, although, it is written in the Bible. "Satan's statement to Eve was recorded by inspiration, but it was not true."[4] Hence, what needs to be considered about the Bible being the inspired word of God or, as some would argue, it being the word of God, is not to say that inspiration is of Divine authority. "Occasionally that is not the case."[5] One can be inspired to write, but that does not mean that the inspired written content is the truth. What must be considered is, the idea of the Bible being the whole word of God, arose from the roots of the early European Christian church. These early European Christians understood Christian theology to be associated with church, money, power, and religious influence over the people. The rise of popes during early Western Christianity perpetuated this idea. Wealth, power, authority, pope and church became bed partners. Therefore, it was believed that all church members were obligated by Divine law to discharge their financial obligations to the church or by church mandates as dictated by the pope. However, what needs to be understood and considered is that the entire Bible is not composed of the word of God, but that it contains the word of God (John 1:19ff). Because of this fact, focus needs to be placed on content, intent and reality; not on rituals, conditions and uncontested traditions. In this way,

---

4 Henry C. Thiessen, <u>Lectures in Systematic Theology</u>, p. 66.
5 Ibid.

the reader will remain open to the ongoing revelations and inspiration of God's words. As a song writer puts it, "please be patient with me, God is not through with me yet." God is not through with His words to us, "*the Holy Spirit...will teach you everything...*" (John 14:26).

For instance, financial support for religious institutions is nothing new and such support was not restricted to tithes. During the temple days of Jesus' era, public taxes were assessed from Jewish men* to support the temple (Mal.3:6,7; Matt.17:24-27; 23:23; Heb.7:8-10). Thus, status, authority and power of the church over the people could be preserved through wealth gotten from the people. This was accomplished by tithing, which in turn was associated with a divinely ordained law, just as church, power, authority and religious influence over the people is associated and synonymous with money. For through tithing, the status of power and authority of the church over the people could be maintained along with the building of the church.

The second and more complex argument is, "...the written form..." is not distinct from "...the Divine voice in the prophet..."[6] Said another way, is what the prophet wrote and spoke of the word of God one and the same? If yes, then the word of God spoken by the prophet is the same as the teachings of God by the prophets (Is. 1:10f; 2:3; 30:9). However, if the word of God spoken by the prophet is not distinct from the written word of God by the prophet, then "...the doctrine of God mediated by the priest,"[7] poses a theological problem (cf. Jer.18:18; Mal. 2:7). The

---

* It must be understood that we are dealing with patriarchal times and people. Therefore, tithing is a function of men only, not women. Tithing is being addressed to the men only!
6 TDNT. (Vol. IV), p. 96: #d.
7 Ibid.

theological problem being: [That which is spoken of God is not at all times what God said or intended (cf. Ex.33: 19f; Nr.12:6-8; 14:13, 14)].

Therefore, what needs to be considered, are prophets and priests the same? And, when we speak of one, do we also speak of the other? More specifically [not including the prophet Malachi] is "the doctrine of God mediated by the priest" the same as the word of God on the lips of the prophet, or, which of the two is the more perfect saying? Or, is what the prophet said that God said the same as what God said? (See Jeremiah 23:23-32 and Chapter 28).

In the case of Malachi, what's left is not a question of the accuracy of the words of Malachi, but whether Malachi is prophet, priest, or an appellation being used as a divine instrument of God to address an issue pertinent only to Old Testament experiences? The introduction to Malachi, (NRSV 1977) and The Jerome Biblical Commentary, (1968) has this to say; "Nothing is known about the person of Malachi... may be only an appellation based on 3:1."

Hence, Malachi may rather be a designation simply because Malachi means my messenger (3:1). What, therefore, remains is that messenger could very well be an appellation for any priest (3:1) or prophet whose function is to teach God's word to a nation rapidly decaying spiritually, specifically, the "majority in Israel..."[8] [If Malachi is an appellation, then he stands outside of his prophecy. However, if Malachi is a person, then he is including himself in his prophecy]. Hence, what follows is, tithing could be for a selected group of people, a "majority in Israel" spoken by Malachi and not just for any and everybody: *"...therefore you, O sons of Jacob, are*

---

8 TDNT. (Vol. IV), p. 179: #2.

not consumed..." (3:6). They are not consumed, if they turn to God with a full measure of devotion to include justice, and that God is merciful to His chosen. But, because the sons of Jacob are not turning to God with a full measure of devotion, God through Malachi says of them *"...you are robbing Me:"(8),* and because of this, "You are cursed with a curse, ...the whole nation of you" (9). (Italics are my emphasis.)

Hence, the contest is not whether God's word finds a higher level of accuracy on the lips of prophet or priest, or whether the accuracy of God's word is equal on the lips of both. Rather, the case in Malachi is tithing, addressed as an O.T. issue between God and Israel (sons of Jacob), who are the select "majority in Israel."

Tithing, as required by law, is an ongoing O.T. concern between God and Israel. Malachi is addressing an O.T. issue on tithing as it evolved and pertains to God and Israel beginning in the days of Abram and Melchizedek (Gen.14:17-20); continuing with Jacob's promise to God for safe passage to his father's house (Gen.28:18-22); and finally, according to the requirements of votive law in (Lev.27:1-3); and services rendered in (Num. 18:21-24). What is being addressed in Malachi is that resolution and reconciliation between God and the "sons of Jacob" (3:6), cannot be accomplished with tithes alone. Righteousness and reconciliation, is the key to tithing (2:17-3:4ff), and has been the key to reconciliation since the days of Abram and Melchizadek. Hence, accuracy of scripture interpretation, understanding, time, event, purpose and persons involved (sons of Jacob) are key to understanding Mal.3:6-12.

Yet, a final point (Mal.3:9) needs to be considered, and

that is the word "cursed." What must be understood in (9) is that the people are not being cursed, rather, this is a warning from God that their crops will fall under the locust (11). It is the curse of crop failure (Gen.3:17ff), not a cursed people. Not only that, but persons already exist in a state of a self-imposed curse, if they cheat on God (Mal.1:14). However, God's first option is to bless Jacob (Mal.3:6) in order to avoid having hardships heaved upon them (4:5).

But, a third and final point should also be considered which may even shed some light on the first point pertaining to the sameness of the word of God and that of the prophet who speaks the word of God. When the prophets of old were inspired to write, did the original inspiration extend to translations of the Bible? Said another way, *does the original inspiration extend to translations and/or does the translations advance the idea of the original text to the current status of the cultures of today; not to lessen the original spiritual message, but rather to tax our spiritual insights to search for the truth in the original inspiration?*

Third Insight:

THE FAILINGS OF THE PRIESTS

What needs addressing from the above are two things. First, the 'any priest syndrome,' and secondly, "...the seriousness of Divine judgment on the majority of Israel."[9] The struggle going on is one of God's great love for Israel (Mal.1:2) contrasted with Israel's despite for God (2:6-14). Often what we fail to realize is that God's desire and capacity to love us, far outstrips our capacity to love Him and others. In light of this struggle, it becomes the priests'

---

9 Ibid, p.179.

responsibility to convey God's love to Israel by assuming liability for Israel's behavior (1:6 & 2:1,2). Israel had lost sight of practicing justice, mercy and faith and had rather ritualized the practice of tithing as the most important means of worship (Matt. 23:23,24). Thus, the job of the priests became one for which their mediations between Israel and God must be about teaching the justice of God and His mercies towards Israel. However, the great issue involved is the failings on part of the priests to do this. The priests were not reliable in their just mediations. What Malachi does (as a priest type representation) is to address divine issues surrounding the business of tithing while focusing on the acceptability and conditions for tithing. The conditions and what is acceptable for tithing is brought out in these words, "you have turned aside from my statues and have not kept them," (3:7). Again, tithing has no meaning aside from the fulfilling of the whole Law.

Therefore, the gist of the matter is this: The priests are failing in their responsibilities in teaching a specific "majority in Israel" and they are failing in such ways as "…turn(ing) aside from my [God's] statutes…" (Mal. 2:8). Israel was not fulfilling the whole Law while tithing and they were also profaning their relationship with God by bringing to God as an offering "…what has been taken in violence or is lame or sick…" (1:13), including violating the basic rules of tithing (3:8). They took the spirit of tithing out of tithing. Put more succinctly, they were sloppy worshippers and thus not all tithes were acceptable to God and under certain circumstances tithing is profane.

Because of this, will a man "rob God," not only pertains to profane tithing, offerings and sloppy worship habits as discussed above, but also robbing God is "…by keeping back the stipulated offerings…, …a novel in prophetic preaching...in that...usually God insisted that He did not need the people's gifts, (cf. Is. 43:23; Ps. 50:7-15),"[10] see also (Is.1:11-15), especially if it is rotten or given in sloppy worship form. What can be concluded from this action is that the people's gifts were either profane, which is robbing God, and/or that God does not burden us to give to Him what is rightfully His, (2 Chr. 29:10-16). Hence, the priests had not only profaned tithing by violating the rules of tithing, but also failed in every case to assume responsibility of correct teachings on the law of tithing as it is tied to the whole law; for it is written, "Curse be every one who does not abide by all things written in the book of the law and do them." (Gal. 3:10b).

Thus, in light of the failings of the priest to teach the acceptability and conditions for tithing according to the law, the people of God are to return to God with a full measure of devotion (Mal.3:7), along with their tithes (3:10), as required by law (7); however, not the law of the Ten Commandments (because tithing is not mentioned in the Ten Commandments), but a law (maintenance law), inferior to the Commandments. These are laws that were put in place *until the Messiah comes* (Gal. 3:10-26). The law was not only "...our custodian until Christ came, that we might be justified by faith" (24), but the law also functioned as acts of devotion to God as part of God's statutes and we are no longer under the law *with the coming of Jesus* (25); (also see Gal. 4:4,5).

Yet, Jesus came not to destroy these laws or the tithing relationship established between God and Israel. But rather He came to knit together their relationship on a spiritual level and less on that of legalities so that the law according to Galatians would not be a curse to anyone living under

---

10 The Jerome Biblical Commentary, 23:67.

the law then and now (3:10-13). Prior to the coming of Jesus, this law was confined to the human practices of religious rituals and highly stylized worship events. Under this system, everybody was cursed simply because, "For all who rely on works of the law are under a curse;" (10a). Hence, tithing also fell under the same curse "of the law." For to violate the law in part, is to make void the whole law.

The coming of Jesus and the Old Testament laws on tithing could not meet the requirements of the New Testament spirit of giving. Tithing could not knit God and his people together in a spiritual alliance no more than could the law. Hence, tithing under the "curse of the law" gave way to giving under grace; "For the law was given through Moses; grace and truth came through Jesus Christ," (Jn. 1:17). Jesus came to lift us above these fixed mundane religious practices that brought a curse upon them so as it would not be a curse upon us. He came to lift us up into the spiritual realm of worship whereby one can in fact experience the abundance of life for which life offers in the freedom of the spirit and not be confined to the limitations of law and the legalities of tithing. For life lived in a spiritual relationship with God while living in the flesh is life lived in abundance. Such abundance of life can only be experienced in the spirit while still confined in the flesh, (cf. Matt.5:7; John 10:10). This type of freedom and life in abundance could never be realized within the confines of law. Legalities and the practices of religious rituals are tied to the legalities of tithing, all falling under the "curse of the law" (Gal. 3:13). What's the purpose of going back under the curse?

Tithing, therefore, was not important to Jesus because tithing confined the tithers to the "curse of the law." Not only that but the tither becomes bonded to the remaining

90% of their possessions, if not all 100% as discussed above. This must have been repulsive to Jesus because tithes do not liberate one from their bondage to money as does the gospel of Jesus Christ which totally liberates one from all earthly possessions: "...You cannot serve God and Mammon" (Matt.6:24b; KJV), see also, 19:16-24 including the law (Gal. 4:4). Tithes were ritualized acts of devotion to God (Lev. 27:26-30; Num. 18:21-24), as they were also acts of men received by and for mortal men (Heb. 7:8) and for mortal purposes.

Because of this, tithing could not give the tithers full measure of an abundant life to be experienced in the spirit of liberation and freedom while still confined to the practices of the flesh and the law. This is Jesus' point to the Pharisees in Matt. 23:24 when He called them "blind guides." Arnold G. Fruchtenbaum's comment on this pericope is, "Why risk doing great damage to the body of Christ and great harm to the integrity of the scripture, when what is at stake are essentially cultural and traditional practices, many of which were already corrupted by the time of Christ?"[11] They were not free spirits. They were in confinement, as well as, "cultural and traditional practices" under the law. Jesus' gospel is about liberation from the flesh and possessions, even from the element of profanity, as we have already seen and we will deal with it again below.

Tithing also, as mentioned above, is an O.T. maintenance law used as an incorporated worship tool in a devotional relationship with God. It was also a means to pay the Levite Priests for their responsibility and service to the temple, "the Levites shall have no inheritance among the

---

11 Fruchtenbaum, ISRAELOGY, The Missing Link In Systematic Theology, pp. 919-920.

people of Israel, " because they will "bear their own iniquity..." (Nr. 18:21ff).

Yet, the priests failed in their conceptual understanding of the differences between 'the abundant life to be experienced in the spirit' and that of living a highly restricted life within the boundaries of strict religious practices and the rigid laws pertaining to tithing. In their practices and teachings of the latter, rituals were taught and emphasized over truth. Israel had inherited from these religious practices, bondage and not freedom in the spirit of God. This caused the people to "...turn aside from the way...and many to stumble" (Mal. 2:8). They even stumbled in their tithing (3:7,8), by tithing profane foods (1:12,13).

What further needs addressing in light of the failings of the priests to teach God's law accurately is further highlighted in Matt.23:23. The "woes" of Jesus "attacks the teachings of the scribes and Pharisees"[12] on tithing. In other words, the scribes and Pharisees' emphases on tithing negated the "weightier matters of the law" so that in (vs. 24) Jesus shows how very insignificant tithing is in the face of "neglecting...justice and mercy and faith." Verse 24, too often ignored in the face of (vs. 23), is in fact the main point to grasp in order to understand (vs.23). For (vs. 24) points to Jesus' "final touch of ridicule"[13] of the scribes and Pharisees in their failings to teach accurately God's Law. For in the hyperbolic language of Jesus, just as they let the camel slip through the strainer but managed to trap out the gnat, so it was that the scribes and the Pharisees managed to let tithing slip through the strainer, trapping out "justice and mercy and faith."

---

12 JBC, 43:159.
13 Ibid.

Thus, the scribes and Pharisees' reasoning for tithing was irrational in the face of (vs. 24). For just as irrational as it was for them to consume the camel and throw away the gnat to keep from choking, to Jesus, it is equally irrational to tithe and at the same time throw away "the weightier matters of the law, justice and mercy and faith." In both instances, not only are they blind but they will no doubt, as implied, choke from their show of public ostentatious tithing complete with their spiritual ignorance of the "weightier matters of the law."

Fourth Insight:

TITHING AND THE LAW vs. THE SPIRIT OF GIVING IN LOVE

To maximize the requirements of tithing over justice, mercy and faith is to minimize the maximum importance of sharing and fully participating in the spirit of giving in love.

After one has reached a certain level of spiritual development, their service to the Lord must also reach new heights. There are basic requirements to becoming saved for which after these requirements have been met, one moves on to higher spiritual heights. One realizes that one does not move on to these heights because of requirements, but rather because of where they are in their spiritual maturity. To say it another way, after having been saved for a period of time, one ought be saved enough to be teachers and leaders, although this is not always the case. But what must be realized, in keeping up with their spiritual development, one should, "...leave the elementary doctrine of Christ and go on to maturity" (Heb. 6:1). This, therefore, is the beginning of Christian maturity.

Simply put, at this level of spiritual maturity, a Christian gives service to the Lord not because of requirement, but because they enjoy it. A Christian is committed by 'joy' not by law or requirement. Therefore, it becomes by far more important to give from the spirit of "justice and mercy and faith," than to tithe by reason of some religious requirement, ritual, or mandate of law put in place because of people's sins, sloppy worship habits, profane tithing practices and an overall lack in their personal commitment to the joy of giving. Sin caused the Israelites to fall short of their minimum requirements of growing spiritually after their entry into a covenant relationship with God; (see 2 Chr. 7:14). They substituted their minimum requirement of growing spiritually, with paying the minimum requirement of tithing. *Tithing is therefore a result of sin, not a by-product of joy and growing in the spirit of God.* One does not grow spiritually by being limited to the borders of tithing. Rather, one grows spiritually within the unlimited boundaries of giving. It is a joy to give but a legal obligation to tithe because of sin. Tithing, therefore, in the Old Testament, is because of sin and is thus tied to the legalities of law being played out in the religious orders of the Israelites because of their lack in spiritual maturity. It was a means for which the Israelites could preserve their covenant relationship with God as a community. Jesus had not yet come with His gospel of salvation (Luke 4:18) for which tithing was not reckoned as a means to an end of relating to or being with the Lord forever.

Furthermore, tithing is tied to events of the O.T. and not the N.T., i.e.; the first harvest of the land is tithe, the conversion of property into money to pay for the Levites' service in the Temple, and etc. Giving, as introduced in the New Testament with the coming of Jesus, is tied to love not events pertaining to property or the legalities of the law. One gives freely, not because they are obligated by a legal or divine injunction mediated by a priest but rather because joy is experienced in giving. Giving binds one in Christian love rather than tithing which tends to bond one to their property.

Hence, cheerful giving in the N.T. is the spiritual designator used to produce economical equity as opposed to the O.T. laws on the legalities attached to tithing. One's spiritual worth and maturity is measured in their cheerful giving, "...the Lord loves a cheerful giver" (2 Cor. 9:7), not a partially law abiding tither. Hence, when one gives, it is done because one wants and loves to give and not because they are required to participate in the rituals of paying minimum sums of monies to the church. From a Jewish perspective, tithing is an O.T. law and not a N.T. love. Tithing takes root, reaches full maturity and dies in the O.T. Rabbi Melvin Glazer had this to say: *"We have a dues structure: If you join the synagogue, this is how much you're going to pay per family per year; we don't pass the plate and we don't insist on tithing. Also, Christianity is based on love, while Judaism is based on justice; we believe that justice is the way to love...."*[14]

Hence, the whole notion of the O.T. concerning tithing is tied to justice and legalities, which to O.T. thought is love. The whole notion of love in the N.T. is tied to grace and giving (Jn. 3:16). "The Lord loves a cheerful giver;" this, and a host of other N.T. quotes on the whole business of love, is built around N.T. themes of giving, "It is better to give than it is to receive" (Acts 20:35). To hear the whole matter, tithing, justice, law and love finds kinship in the O.T., just as giving, forgiving, love and grace finds kinship in the N.T. What is common to both is mercy and faith.

14 Princeton Alumni (Fall 1992), Melvin Glazer, D. Min. student, Princeton Theological Seminary.

Fifth Insight:

TITHING, GIVINGS and OFFERINGS

If there be any truth to the natural order of domination, or dominating influences, then that which is dominate rules: Sky over earth, heaven over hell or a mere show of force in numbers i.e.; (10>9). In other words, numbers have their merits in domination.

Yet, I need to preface my fifth insight with the foregoing before proceeding. *First and foremost, I do not take issue with anyone who purports the profundity of tithing or the profundity of tithing in the Bible. Furthermore, I respect their understanding of tithing should they understand tithing in accordance with the Bible's views. Should they understand tithing in accordance with how a religious denomination comes to interpret the Bible's views on tithing and in turn impose these views upon their local congregations or individual members, I also respect that approach. But, that's another story at issue with this writer for which much of this paper addresses.*

Secondly, If any person(s) is firmly convicted of tithing, however they came about their conviction, then they should stick with it. I say, stick with it on the premises of (Num. 30:1,2; & Deut. 23:21-23). Finally, I elect to turn to the Bible's views and understanding on tithing. I do this not only in light of what has been discussed, but also in light of the foregoing discussions.

Thirdly, Tithing in the O.T. reflects the larger truth of giving in the N.T. The mistakes often made about tithing are the hortatory and not the explanatory preaching on tithing. More persuasion, cajolery and blandishment is used in the preaching language concerning tithing than that of explicating, elucidating and illuminating. *In preaching, it is much easier to be hortatory than explanatory. The JBC comment on the Trinity can be equally applied to tithing. "For instance, a biblical treatment of the Trinitarian ...passages in the N.T. would reflect the impression of First Century thought on that subject; but a preacher should clarify this imprecision as historically the later Church did. A biblical sermon on a subject like the Trinity should reflect the biblical aspect of a larger truth."[15]*

Hence, when we deal with the distinctive idea of O.T. tithing as found in Mal. 3:8-10, then this pericope ought not be read independently and separately from 3:2,3. For just as, "A biblical sermon on a subject like the Trinity should reflect the biblical aspect of a larger truth," Mal. 3:2,3 in turn reflects for 3:8-10 the biblical aspect of a "larger truth" in the Bible, which is 'giving' that is now realized in the N.T.

The Old Testament reflects a larger truth in the Bible that will come to fulfillment with better understanding in the N.T. What must be realized is that the events of the O.T. are truths for that time, and these truths come to fullness and completion in the N.T. and in the being of Jesus; who He is, what He did and what He said.

Tithing, in the Bible, is by far not the most profound biblical theme of the Bible. ***The Bible has only one profound theme and that is salvation!:*** (O.T.; 2Chr. 7:14, Eze. 18:32: N.T; Luke 4:18-21, John 3:16). Any and everything else is subordinate to this purposeful and unique theme of the Bible. In view of this, tithing is not N.T. It was not originated in the N.T., neither is it germane

---

15 JBC, 71:99.

to the same. In the N.T. there is not even a place for it. The times tithing is mentioned in the N.T., all have their references to the O.T., the place of its origin and demise, (see page 75). At best, in the N.T. era, we can assume tithing to be tolerated but not a requirement. Besides, while living in the N.T. era we must be careful not to perpetuate the O.T. attitudes towards the legalities of tithing and having them clashing with the N.T. attitudes of giving which is characteristic of the spirit of giving in the N.T. Tithing and giving are not the same.

I had mentioned above something about the natural order of domination. From a numerical point-of-view, should one count the numbers of acceptable and most common ways mentioned in the Bible for which one can pay their gifts to God, they will come up with three, namely: *Tithing, Offerings and Giving.* Of the acceptable three, the numerical approximates would be as follows:

> *Tithing,* in all forms is mentioned in the Bible about 40 times. Of these times, it is mentioned in the O.T. 32 times and eight (8) in the N.T. Of these eight (8) times mentioned in the N.T., five (5) are found in the book of Hebrews, for which all are in direct reference to the O.T.

> *Offerings,* in all forms are mentioned about 1,400 times. Of these times, offerings are mentioned about 1,333 times in the O.T. and about 67 in the N.T.

> *Giving,* in all forms, is mentioned about 1,700 times. Of these times, giving is mentioned about 1,300 in the O.T., and about 400 in the N.T.

To briefly summarize, the above in terms of all forms of oblations to God mentioned in the Bible are about 3,140 times. The O.T. claims about 2,665 of these times and the N.T. 475 times. We learn two things from this survey. First, that the O.T. over the N.T. houses the most interest in paying oblations to God in some materialistic form; and that secondly, the least preferred method of giving oblations to God is in the pre-determined amount of *tithing*. Not only is *tithing* the least mentioned method of paying oblations in the Bible, but there still remains another concern about *tithing* in the Bible that is a devastating blow *against it*. For instance, in the Bible, *tithing* has some very strong negatives against it:

- In 1 Sam. 8:15,17 *tithing* is one of the abuses Israel is to suffer under a king.
- In Gen. 14ff, *tithing* is connected with booty gained in war.
- Amos 4:4ff, Amos condemned *tithing* as a form of abuse. Israel was oppressing the common and poor people yet would offer *tithing* to the Lord while doing these evils.
- Matt. 23:23, and Luke 11:42, Jesus condemns the Pharisees for their lack of a sense of proportion and spiritual understanding with regard to what was important in religious observances when it comes to tithing.

Offerings, on the other hand, have its preferences over *tithing*; however, offerings are strongly associated with sacrifices as we noted in the story of Abraham and Isaac; and in (2 Chr. 29ff), where live stock are being offered up as sacrifices. There are also wheat and cereal *offerings* of lesser sacrificial status.

Finally, there is *giving*. *Giving*, is numerically the preferred method of paying oblations to God. Yet, this is not the only superior advantage *giving* has over *offerings and tithing*. In *giving*, as opposed to the other two methods, there is no pre-determined amount to give. Not only that, but *giving* is associated with David's prayers of blessing the Lord (1 Chr. 29:6-14). The people gave willingly after "consecrating" themselves. Hence, it would appear that when one gives, it is done not because of requirements but rather that one wishes and loves to give. One is not bonded to their wealth in giving. Thus, in light of this prayer, *offerings* take a back seat to *giving* while *tithes* are not even mentioned.

Furthermore, consideration should be given to yet another dimension of giving. This consideration should be one of giving for the joy of giving. The Bible uses the adjective, "cheerful" giving. Thus, when one gives it is not done because of a requirement but because one desires and wants to give, also because one loves to give. Giving cheerfully involves love (2 Cor. 9:7; Rom. 12:6-10) whereas, *offerings* and *tithing* do not (Isaiah 1ff).

In summary, giving as used in the N.T., is in the <u>spirit</u> not in the legalities of the Law. In the Bible, giving is the preferred standard of demonstrating one's spirituality in general. Giving, more often than not and more than any of the other two methods of paying oblations to God, is used as the more acceptable standard of a meaningful relationship with God for which in turn, God will respond favorably to the giver. For this reason, giving is a spiritual designator, which stands aloof in a class of the other two methods. On the other hand, tithing in the Bible is always tied to the legalities of the law.

Thus, from a N.T. point-of-view, we do well to maximize the importance of giving cheerfully because of who we are and because we love the Lord and the works of the Lord. The songwriter wrote: "Give of your best to the Master" not tithe in accordance to the law for the Master; because in the lyrics of another song we sing the testimony of the Master, "I gave, I gave my life for thee," which is a fitting testimony to (John 3:16). Yet the lyrics continue with this challenge, "What hast thou given me?" Let not our response to this challenging invitation be, I gave, I gave the best of me. I gave my tithes for Thee. Tithing is not one's best, it is their least! Requirements of one should not be in the mood of the least but rather in the mode of the best. When the least is given, great expectations in return may be the norm, but there is yet to follow the consequences of the reality for paying the least and expecting the most.

Frank Stagg observes that, "Stewardship" (of which many churches interpret tithing to be a central part) "in the New Testament is always person-centered. Attention is never fixed upon money and things as such. Collection of money is never made an end in itself. New Testament interest is in God, the Christian, and his fellow man." He continues, "The measure of giving is always personal, never quantitative," thus, "Jesus repeatedly warned against the tyranny of the material" and that, "One must choose between God and mammon (Matt.6:24)."[16]

David H. Stern summed up tithing in these words, "...the main point in this [tithing]... is that one should properly order one's priorities so as to live a life pleasing to God."[17]

But, hear the whole matter. The whole self and all that we

---

16 F. Stagg, New Testament Theology, p. 285 f.
17 D. H. Stern, Jewish New Testament Commentary, p. 71.

possess is the best that we can give in the service of the Lord; after all, did the Lord do any less for us? Thus!

I wonder where I would be,
had the Lord not preached,
but just tithe
His gospel to me?
I wonder what would be all the fuss,
had the Lord Jesus not given,
but just
Tithe His life for us?

August, 1996

Chapter
Five

SPIRITUAL BLINDNESS

Mark 8:22-26; John 9:24-34

Blindness in the Bible is viewed as a bewildering human defect standing in the way of one's salvation. To be blind is not only considered an abnormal physical condition but is also perceived as a serious spiritual defect – the condition of the former being analogous to the existing state of the latter. For example: In Mark, to be physically blind is so serious a condition that one who is blind, is thought also to have no understanding. In John's gospel, spiritual blindness is seeing without understanding. Matthew and Luke are similar to Mark and John in that all carry the same notion of seeing without understanding. Compared with today's notion of this type of spiritual blindness, the idea would be synonymic with the 'I-see-it-but-don't-believe-it' cliche.

However, imbedded in the condition of spiritual blindness are three self-willed negative human characteristics for which the Bible truly frowns upon:
- Ignorance
- Lack of understanding
- Ego tripping

For a brief moment, let's look at all three:

Ignorance

Ignorance, as a condition of spiritual blindness, is akin to the Adam and Eve story. Eve was ignorant of the fact that built into the knowledge of evil is the sin of temptation. In her one-on-one dialogue with the master deceiver, Satan, he never told her that built into evil is the unseen sin of temptation. Not only that, but there are also consequences in just knowing evil – one of which is yielding to it. What Eve did not see was the price one must pay in just having knowledge of evil. For just as the knowledge of sin and evil carries the seed of temptation, yielding to temptation carries an even greater price. For the consequences in just knowing evil is in itself an unbearable test, not to mention the price for yielding to temptation. For yielding can cost one their life and loss of their salvation. Yielding is an evil to resist. The results might not be immediately apparent but there are both short and long-range consequences having both far reaching and long term effects, as in the Adam and Eve story. Eve yielded and it was downhill all the rest of the way.

Lack of Understanding

What Eve failed to understand is that having the ability to discern the difference between good and evil is not the same as resisting evil. What she lost in the process of wanting to know good and evil was the ability to maintain self-control and of using common sense. It takes self-control, good common sense and spiritual maturity in order not to practice and do the evil we know; and much more of the same, in order not to think and meditate on it. For when we sin, something of the use of good common sense is lost in the process. For instance, after Adam and Eve sinned, they could not even understand that they could not hide from God in His own garden.

Ego Tripping

We find that neither Adam nor Eve wanted to accept the blame for their wrong but instead, they blamed each other and Satan. They were too busy protecting their egos. To say it another way, the ever present nebulous population-of-people, the so-called 'theys,' are the ones who made them do wrong. In other words, Adam blamed God and Eve, and Eve blamed Satan. Thus, in blaming and accusing the other is not only spiritually blinding to the blamer and accuser but it also feeds the behavior of spiritual blindness. Over a period of time, blaming and accusing blinds one to their own shortcomings. Blaming and accusing also closes the doors to effective communication - or for that matter, any communication at all. Spiritual blindness destroys communion between spouses and with God. When communion was broken with God, Adam and Eve broke communion between themselves. For after Adam and Eve sinned, they did not talk to one another. They were busy building walls of differences between themselves, trying to hide their nudity from each other by sewing fig leaves for a covering. But for what reason? They had been walking around naked in front of each other all this time, why hide now from one another? Spiritual blindness causes guilt and shames the body!

The rationale for blaming, which is not rational at all, was their sin. Sin in return causes one to become spiritually blind. Spiritual blindness, therefore, causes one to do irrational things. It causes one to lose respect for self and for their loved ones. It causes one to become intolerant of the other. It causes one not to be satisfied with their own lives. Eve was not satisfied with the dumb mistake she made, neither was Adam for listening to her. The result is that they, like us, wanted to hide from their stupidity. No one wants to expose their weaknesses, especially if it could have been avoided after receiving proper instructions. In cases of husbands and wives where communication between them is broken, for whatever reasons, they may find it extremely difficult to survive the marriage vow, "until death do we part." Why? Because the husband and wife expectation of each other does not take under serious consideration the frailties of their own individual weaknesses. It is a sad commentary that today the average life expectancy of marriage in America is only two years and the chief cause of marital conflict which heads the list of divorces is a lack of communication.

Spiritual blindness is also forgetfulness. For example, when we formally celebrate our black heritage only in the month of February, we treat our heritage as a novelty, which is theatrically celebrated once a year and then shelved to be forgotten for the next eleven months. But we should not make theatrics out of the legacy of sacrifices paid by our foreparents so that we might enjoy the freedoms of today. The wisdom, not the shame, drawn from the sacrifices made for us by them should not be ritualized annually but rather realized daily. Such an unique heritage, as our black heritage, bears recognition throughout the entire year. It is ours to keep alive daily because as James Weldon Johnson wrote...

Stony the road we trod, bitter the chast'ning rod,
Felt in the days when hope unborn had died;
Yet with a steady beat, have not our weary feet,
Come to the place for which our father's sighed?

We have come, over a way that with tears
has been watered.
We have come, treading our path thro' the
blood of the slaughter.
Out from the gloomy past, till now we stand at last,
Where the white gleam of our bright star is cast.

Such a heritage as this deserves a daily vanguard because we know that many of us, because of our ignorance of our history, are ashamed of it. Therefore, those many more who do not forget the black experience in America captured above in the words of James Weldon Johnson, must become the vanguards of our heritage. Together we must face the truth of the matter that although the task is hard, we must teach hard and not slacken in the importance of teaching our black heritage in order to enlighten the ignorant. For the sake of our future, we must be relentless in our teachings so that unborn generations might grow up into the enlightenment of a proud heritage and not join the ranks of heritage-ignorance, and shame. It is for us to keep alive our heritage continuously, because no matter how bitter it was, it is our only commonly shared experience in North America that gives black solidarity. Furthermore, our heritage is a hope of the future. For from the ashes of slavery rose a new creation which we all share. From the burned out ashes of slavery rose a marvelous black intellect as a testimony to this new creation. This testimony is, as James Weldon Johnson said, "our bright star(s)," captured in the glowing historical accomplishments of persons like: Dr. Daniel Hale Williams First heart operation; Benjamin Banneker Invented the Almanac and laid the plans for Washington, D.C.; Frederick McKinley Jones Invented refrigeration; Granville T. Woods Invented the electric railways; Norbert Rillieux Invented sugar refining; Ida B. Wells She, before the turn of the century, was the first black person not to give up her seat to whites in the white section of public transportation. Dr. Ida Gray First black woman dentist in America. Dr. Susan McKinney Steward First black woman pediatrician and GYN in USA. Elijah J. McCoy, he is the real McCoy. He invented the self-lubricating machines while still in motion. We must, therefore, understand that spiritual blindness is a form of forgetfulness that destroys everything about a person; their history, heritage and their spirituality. Unless we remember the marvelous black intellect that rose from the ashes of slavery that gave us our heritage, we will be swallowed up in a sea of forgetfulness – the destroyer of the soul.

But what must be looked at in more detail in dealing with spiritual blindness is the consequences of knowing both good and evil. For we have already discovered that there are consequences in just knowing evil and sin. We have discovered that built into the knowledge of evil and sin is temptation. For in knowing good and evil we are predisposed to a problem that will defeat us. That problem is; we want to act alone while working through temptation's snares. We do this without consulting God and others for help. Sin causes one to become proud and individualistic. But to act this way is to head for trouble. For without God, we have neither ability to control nor the sensibility to navigate around temptations.

Thus, what results is our understanding is in what we see and what we see is like that of a camera that snaps sights, but does not capture insights. We see, but we do not understand. We see without realizing all the bad and inescapable consequences that come with performing the act we visualize. We see but we do not comprehend. We see wrong, but we have no defense against it. We see evil, yet we do not recognize or realize its long range devastating effects. 1Tim.5:24 said it just right, "The sins of some men are conspicuous, pointing to judgment, but the sins of others appear later." "We see through a glass dimly," records the writer in 1Cor.13; but when our eyes clear, our sins are often too deeply embedded in us to do anything about them. Thus, is the nature of spiritual blindness. We lose control for we cannot "beat the devil running;" we lose sensibility in that, "temptation sweeps over our souls and sunlight is hidden from view." We lose common sense because our sins have overtaken us and it is too late to do anything except suffer through them. We are caught-up in temptations' snares.

There is a story told about **The Garden of Love and Understanding** which seem to put in focus something about having sufficient understanding in order to defeat spiritual blindness. It is the kind of Love and Understanding spoken of in 1Cor.13ff. The story tells of three travelers in search of the path that led to the flower garden of Love and Understanding. When they found it, the *first traveler* plucked a honeysuckle, inhaled the sweet fragrance and then cast it aside. The first traveler then discussed with his other two traveling companions his own understanding of Love and Understanding and concluded that Love and Understanding must be sweet; then he went about his way. But soon the honeysuckle withered by the roadside and died.

The *second traveler* plucked a beautiful orchid, only to admire it. It was beautiful, delicate and softly colored. He discussed with his companions that Love and Understanding must be like this orchid, beautiful and delicate to behold. However, like the first traveler, he did not care for the flower; he only enjoyed its beauty for a moment in time and like the first traveler, cast it aside. It too, soon withered and died due to a lack of care.

The *third traveler* dug up a rose bush but he was pricked many times by its thorny stems. Yet he planted it in his garden, pruned and cared for it. Though it continued to prick him many times while he cared for it, the rose plant grew into a beautiful fragrant rose bush to give him continuous enjoyment of lasting beauty.

There is a moral behind this story. It's a story of redemption after suffering and reward after struggle. The *first traveler* threw away the opportunity to get Love and Understanding through a superficial understanding of what they mean. What he did was to tell others about what he felt about Love and Understanding. His brief encounter with his flower of life led him to believe that Love and Understanding must be sweet and that it requires no effort on his part to maintain such a sweet fragrance. In other words, people like these do not understand the effort it takes in keeping a sound relationship intact. They are but children on the road of Life. They are quick to express how they feel about the first experience they encounter. They are immature, loosely attached to values, flighty, defensive, quick to point out the faults of others, poor listeners and highly intolerant of the feelings of others. They take from life but contribute little to nothing to living. Few are able to attain and none are able to sustain.

The *second traveler* in his brief encounter with his flower of life only gets a taste of Love and Understanding. He is not mature enough to follow through with care. These are the ones who see "in a mirror dimly." They only see part of the total picture and could care little about the rest. They are uncaring and pretentious people who take an apathetic approach to life. They have no interest in a relationship beyond that for which they cannot achieve personal gain. They tend to maintain distant and tenuous relationships. Long term commitment and sacrifice has no meaning to them.

But the *third traveler* reaped the fullness of Love and Understanding. For with patience and care, he was able to accept the scars that come with living, and in turn he reaped the full enjoyment of life. He reaped the life Jesus spoke of when He said, "I came that you might have life and have it more abundantly."

The point to be made is that spiritual blindness can cause

us to not recognize our daily blessings. A song writer best expressed this when he wrote, "Everyday is a day of thanksgiving" while yet another responded in kind, "The Lord is blessing me right now!"

Spiritual blindness also causes one to have what I call a Peter Syndrome. A Peter Syndrome causes one to try and make things happen according to how they imagine they should happen. They dwell on how things ought to be, not how they really are.

We remember the story in Mark when Jesus was teaching Peter that the Son of Man must suffer, be rejected by all the 'church folk' of that day, be killed then on the third day, be raised. We also remember Peter's reaction to Jesus when he called Jesus aside to rebuke Him for saying that He would die. As far as Peter was concerned, dying was not a part of the deal in the ministry of Jesus. Truly the Master did not come to die behind all His good doings and teachings. What a waste! It just ought not to be! But in an instant, Jesus rebuked Peter and said, "get behind me Satan." In an instant, Jesus salvages Peter from his spiritual blindness. In an instant, Jesus showed Peter clearly the difference between how things really are and what Satan would have us to believe in our unwitty imagination: Get behind Me Satan! For the truth of the matter is that the Son of Man will be killed...Get behind Me Satan! The truth of the matter is that the Son of Man came not to be served, but to serve even to the extent of giving His life for the ransom of many...Get behind Me Satan! The truth of the matter is this. Had not the Son of Man died for your sins and mine, we would yet be agonizing in our hopelessness without knowing anything about the joy of our salvation. Had not Jesus died who else could have saved us from sin's jaws of death?

But thank God, just as Jesus opened the eyes of Peter that Peter might see the light of his own salvation, the light of our salvation came on that third day after Calvary. The Prophet Isaiah prophesized it and the Apostle Paul realized it that in Jesus;

"Death is swallowed up in victory,
O grave, where is thy victory?
O death, where is thy sting?
In Jesus we come to know that there is someone
who can help:
Jesus is the answer to every question,
He is the solution to every problem,
The yes in every no and the right in every wrong;
He is the up in every down, the make-up in every
break-up,
The hope for the hopeless, the lost and found department
for every lost soul,
The anonymous healer for every alcoholic and to every
drug addict,
He is the only cure!

If spiritual blindness is separating you from God,
Try Jesus!
If you cannot see your daily blessing, Try Jesus!
If spiritual blindness is causing you to have a Peter
Syndrome, Try Jesus!
Jesus is the reason for living!"

Thanks be to God, who gives us the victory through our Lord Jesus Christ.

February 18, 1996

Chapter
Six

LET'S GET MARRIED!

Genesis 2:18-3:7

In reading the third chapter of Genesis, it does not take long to discover there is trouble in the Garden of Eden – the birthplace of humanity and the honeymoon capital of the world. Yet, it is difficult to realize that all the trouble in the world and all the wrongs of humanity seem to stem from this one single act of disobedience committed by Adam and Eve. They ate "from the tree" which God commanded them "not to eat," and caught a bad case of spiritual ptomaine poisoning – a disease so contagious and infectious, that it triggered a worldwide, far reaching epidemic of spiritual sickness that infected all humanity.

Today, you and I are victims caught in the grip of this catastrophic epidemic. Victims born into a sick world covered with oceans of social, psychological and physical sicknesses. Because of these sicknesses unique to humanity, numerous populations of spiritually sick people are born into the world. In turn, these spiritually sick people marry producing numerous populations of *misfit and nonfunctional relationships,* resulting in numerous populations of *worthless and good-for-nothing offspring.*

Sin today is so widespread, that it jars our imaginations. It causes us to wonder did this single act of disobedience really cause all this trouble in the world; wars, rumors of wars, famine, sicknesses, destruction and death? Did it also produce worldwide broken relationships, miscommunications and the destitution of marriages? For example, are all of these ills we experience today the direct results of Adam and Eve's one time act of disobedience? Well, whether or not we answer yes or no, one thing for sure is, the pitfalls in our marriages today can be traced back to similar pitfalls of this first marriage. But, in spite of it all, folks still say, let's get married! Quick to marry because of the pleasure of the booty and not the performance of duty. However, we should not be too quick to marry without considering the sins of Adam and Eve.

The sins of Adam and Eve impact marriage in two phases:
Phase 1, the four areas of sins and faults in us before we marry.
Phase 2, the three principles of sin arising during the marriage.

These we need to consider.

Four areas in Phase 1 prior to marriage
The first and foremost area we must consider is that long before any marriage ever takes place, we are heavily loaded with unresolved sin problems and faults that has long since been deeply rooted in us. Genesis 2 tells us something about this. It reveals to us that in this first marriage a fault already existed in Adam and Eve long before they became one and transgressed God's command as recorded in Genesis 3.

What we have come to realize about Adam in Genesis 2, is that Adam became nothing more after he sinned than what he was before he sinned. To bear witness to this, we read in Romans 5:12, "...sin came into the world through one man..." and (vs.) 19, "...as by one man's disobedience many were made sinners (so by one man's obedience many will be made righteous)." This scripture predicted what proceeded from both men, Adam and Jesus.

First in the case of Jesus, no sin ever existed in Him.

Therefore, sin never came out of Jesus. But in the case of Adam, if sin proceeded from Adam, then he along with Eve were from the very beginning, not innocent. In other words, you cannot extract sin out of that which is sinless, no more than you can extract perfection out of that which is imperfect. Therefore, what Adam was after he transgressed God's words, is what he was before he transgressed God's word, not innocent. Thus, anything that proceeded from Adam had fault. In the beginning, Eve like Adam was not innocent because she came out of Adam.

But, there is a lesson you and I can learn from this first marriage. We can learn that we are nothing more after we marry than what we were before we married. If we had fault in us after we married, then we had fault in us before we married. If we are sinners or sinners saved by grace after we marry, then we were sinners or sinners saved by grace before we married. In other words, marriage does not in anyway change us into the status of perfection. If we were imperfect before we married, we will also be imperfect after we are married. In other words, like Adam and Eve, we are nothing more after we marry than what we were before we married and that is, we are not innocent of sin.

The second area to consider is this: Anyone that has prohibitions and limits placed on him by God has the knowledge of sin, the potential to sin and the nature of sin.

Therefore, long before the so-called fall in Genesis 3 took place, while Eve was yet a part of the rib of Adam, it was already anticipated in Genesis 2, that Adam along with Eve together had in them the seed to sin. Their sin from the beginning was the weakness of the flesh. The writer of Genesis 2:16-17 knew this. For he makes it very clear to anyone who reads this, that Adam and Eve were made perfectly aware of all the prohibitions in the Garden of Eden given them by God while Eve was yet in the rib of Adam. We read this warning from God to Adam along with Eve that "...in the day you eat of the tree" of the knowledge of good and evil, "you will die." In other words, had not Eve sinned first Adam would have, because Adam was made an androgynous being. We learn from this two things: First, if Adam was faultless (sinless) as Christ, then the knowledge of evil would not have in any way affected him (1 John 3:5-6). Secondly, God placed prohibitions and limitations on Adam, which was indicative of the fact that for Adam to have knowledge of sin was for him to do the sin, and that in itself was sin.

But let's look further into what it means to us for God to set our limits. For example: In the book of Job, God limited the activities of Satan and told Satan just how far he could go with Job because Satan had sin in him before he knew Job.

Moses was prohibited by God from crossing over into the Promised Land. He could see it from a distance but could not enter it because Moses had sinned against God long before he was to enter the Promised Land. You see sin is in us even before we enter into a good event.

Again, the children of the exodus were not all the children who entered into the Promised Land. God raised up a new nation from the exodus because the old nation was prohibited from entering the Promised Land. They were prohibited from entering the Promised Land because the sins of Egypt weighed heavily upon them. In other words, the newly freed nation of Israel, even though they were freed, still had the potential to keep on sinning even after entering the Promised Land. In Genesis 2, Adam had prohibitions and limitations placed on him because he had a fault; **he had the potential and the desire to do the sin he had knowledge of, <u>and that is sin</u>.**

Again, if we look closely at Genesis 2, we will discover something else. We will discover that sin was already present in the very soil of the earth from which God made Adam. For the soil itself needed to be cultivated. We read that the Lord God "put the man in the garden to till it and keep it." In other words, God made a man to "till the soil;" to cultivate it, or prepare it for use because the soil from which Adam was made needed care. It was useless without care. It needed care less it brought forth thorns and thistles. Hence, Adam was not only to have dominance over the earth but he was also responsible for the care of it.

In other words, because Adam was made from the soil, which needed care, Adam, in turn, needed God's care. This is why God placed limits on Adam's activities. For together, Adam and Eve had discovered an evil for which they could not resist and that evil was temptation, because of their weakness in the flesh.

Now to put all this in the light of marriages of today, it would look like this. Just as Adam and Eve were not so innocent prior to their disobedience to God, so it is with us today. No one prior to their marriage is so sinless and faultless that they enter into marriage totally free of both. For fault and sin are present in us from the very beginning. Fault and sin are deeply rooted in the flesh, soul, mind and body of everyone, long before they marry. Not only that, but no matter how nice one may be, the very environment they are born and raised in, is so infested with sin, that they are infected by being exposed to it even if raised in the perfect environment.

In other words, that good little boy who does fine always, will have mud slung on him by the neighborhood bully, or that nice little girl who is a peach out of reach, can hang on that tree just so long before it begins to rot. You see the environment itself will affect us. There are too many things out there for which we are defenseless against. One of them is temptation and the others are the attacks of sin upon our person just from living. We are attacked by sin just for being alive in the flesh. We are victims of environmental sins. We are contending against "the spiritual hosts of wickedness..." "Therefore, we need to put on the whole armor of God, that [we] may be able to withstand in the evil day..." This is why we need the Lord to guide us everyday, as we travel along this narrow way.

The third area to consider is, sin also precedes marriage by means of long-standing independence or living single too long. Genesis 2:18, expands further on the sins that might affect us prior to marriage. Living single too long works against the union in marriage. God said, that it is "not good" that the man should be alone. *The peculiarity of this verse is, this is the only place in the creation story whereby God did something and later said of Himself that what He did was "not good."*

In other words, living single, being alone too long before marriage, does not necessarily work in the best interest of a marriage. While single, we pick-up a lot of deeply rooted habits and behaviors that feed our independence and individuality, which will not go well in a marriage. The environment we create and the company we keep while single does not at all times make a good foundation for marriage.

For example: A number of years ago I counseled a woman

who would not give up the privacy of her bedroom, even after marriage. All of her life she had been taught that her bedroom was her private domain and this was deeply instilled in her. Therefore, after her marriage, she could not allow her husband to share her bedroom or even sleep in the bed with her. She maintained her separate bedroom and the bonding of the marriage never took place. Obviously the marriage did not last.

SIN HAS LONG REACHING EFFECTS. IT STARTS IN OUR SINGLE YEARS LONG BEFORE WE MARRY AND REACHES INTO OUR MARRIAGES. THEREFORE, BEFORE YOU KICK THAT MAN/WOMAN TO THE CURB, YOU'D BETTER FIRST LOOK AT THE FAULT IN YOURSELF.

What we must remember about marriage is this, that when two very different people marry: Number One, both are not without fault prior to their marriage. Number Two, the most important, is a union of two in marriage becomes a transforming experience for both. New persons emerge.

In other words, the marriage itself becomes a person. And if it is a marriage in the Lord, then the marriage is a new person in Christ. And in Christ, 2 Cor.5:17 teaches "...if anyone is in Christ, he is a new creation; the old has passed away, behold, the new has come." 1 John 3:6 teaches that, "No one who abides in Christ sins..." **As Christians, we must ask ourselves has Christ emerged as the new person in the marriage?**

The fourth and final area we need to consider is: The institution of marriage is not a workshop for solutions to previous unresolved problems. Unresolved problems brought to the marriage only cause more hardship in the marriage. You see Adam and Eve had unresolved faults before God punished them for their act of disobedience. One fault they had prior to their marriage, which they carried over into their marriage was that they did not communicate. **Nowhere do you see Adam and Eve ever speaking a single word to each other.** They also must have had other faults because God prohibited their activities while they were yet on their honeymoon (in the Garden of Eden).

One of the many pitfalls of marriage are the hidden unresolved sins, faults, issues and problems we bring to the marriage which should have been resolved before marriage. We create a potentially explosive situation when old unresolved issues are added to new problems arising in the marriage. Those nasty ways, behaviors and attitudes we kept so well hidden in courtship, are now vomited up with no compunction to contain them (no pricking of the conscience). The contrary nature and defiant ways, which were repressed in courtship, now explodes in the marriage. **Getting married will not make anything go away that was there before the marriage. A new person must emerge in a marriage.**

<u>Finally, Phase 2 Three Principles of Sin</u>
Problems arose for Adam and Eve after marriage. For instance, somewhere down the road of their marriage, there arose a contrary spirit between them, and this contrary spirit came out in Eve's dialogue with the serpent. It was a contrary spirit of exclusion. Eve excluded Adam from the most important event in marriage. And that is, making decisions together. Thus, the third Chapter of Genesis is about after the honeymoon. Hence, three principles in need of consideration after marriage.

<u>Principle Number 1</u>: Before you make a judgement call

that involves the well-being of your spouse and the whole family, consider first your own imperfect status. You alone, making a decision from your imperfections can hurt the whole family. We must not assume that Adam and Eve at anytime before the "fall" were so innocent that they were incapable of contemplating transgression, thus making mistakes.

You see, the serpent made the suggestion to Eve, to eat of the tree, and imperfect Eve accepted the suggestion. Out of her imperfection she made an imperfect decision to eat. Her fault was this: In her dialogue with Satan she did not consider her imperfections. Yet, too often we do the same thing. But, the greatest damage we do to our marriages is we wait until after we are married to finger those imperfections in our spouses but not in ourselves. The point to be made is this: Why wait until after the marriage to finger imperfections that have always been there? Imperfections in us have always been there and will always be. The songwriter wrote, *"I have never reached perfection but I've tried...."*

Satan posed the suggestion to Eve to eat of the forbidden fruit in such a way that she would never consider the imperfection of her status. In our marriage, we tend to raise issues with our spouses in such ways as to ignore the imperfection of our own status: 'Why don't you pickup behind yourself??? Well, you first need to look behind your own self......honey'!!!

The story is told of a Moses, but not the same Moses of the Bible. He was an outstanding Rabbi in the synagogue, a Rabbi who had never been exposed to the sins of the world. The time came for him to experience the world as part of his training. Therefore, he was sent forth from the synagogue to put his faith in practice. While he was gone a serious issue arose in the synagogue. One of the Rabbis was called into question about his activities, which required the formation of a Council to consider his case. It was suggested that Moses return and sit in the counsel of judgment. Word was sent out and Moses was contacted. After a period of time, the Council waited outside the doors of the synagogue to greet Moses upon his return. One day while standing outside the doors they saw a figure in a distance and as they watched that figure approach they noticed something strange.

They had identified the figure to be Moses, but strapped to his back was a bag of sand. As Moses approached the doors of the synagogue, the waiting Council noticed a trail of sand leaking from the bag behind him when he came within their presence and stopped. They all stood there for a moment wondering at this strange sight. Eventually one the members of the Council spoke up and asked Moses what was the meaning of this bag strapped to his back leaving the trail of sand behind him. They noticed all the while Moses was standing there the sand was streaming out and a pile was building up behind him. After a few moments Moses responded and said, "These are my sins poured out behind me, I cannot see them but others can."

The first transgression of this first marriage was that Eve did not consider her pile of sand pouring out behind her. She made an imperfect judgment call that would affect not only her relationship with her husband, but the whole human race. From her imperfections...Eve decided for herself that the "tree was good for food"

She decided for herself "it was a delight to the eyes"
She decided for herself that she wanted to be wise

She decided to take of the fruit and eat...

Because of her existing imperfections, for which she failed to consider about herself, she ended up talking to the wrong person.

Principle Number 2: You must not assume that in your idea of choosing the right man or woman for yourself, that they, just because you chose them, are free from transgressing your expectations of them.

In other words, marriage will not fulfill either partner's perfect expectation of the other. Said another way, just because you married me will not cause me to become perfect by your standards. You marrying me has nothing to do with you making me perfect according to your standards.

One of the imperfections, or transgressed expectations, in Adam and Eve's marriage is that they did not communicate with one another. Nowhere do we see in the entire creation story that Adam and Eve ever spoke a single word to each other. Nowhere do they mention the word love between them. You see, there was no communication between them in their relationship. They were in the Garden of Eden, but not in the unity of the spirit of communication. Isn't it strange how husband and wife can furnish their homes and yards so nicely, but cannot talk to one another while living together in the midst of all their niceties. Isn't it strange how we can violate each other's expectations in our marriages by forgetting how to communicate with one another. I find that to be a fault in many relationships, friendship or marriage – we forget how to talk to each other. People don't know the difference between a monologue and a dialogue in relationships. Many couples don't even know what to say to each other, after they marry:

- I don't even know what to say to you anymore...
- I can't talk to you anymore...
- You ain't the same person I married... No! Neither are you!

In other words, just because you chose them as your mate does not mean they were free from resisting your expectations of them. What must be considered, the weakness is not only in your spouse for transgressing your expectations of them, but is also in you for thinking they would live up to your expectations of them.

Principle Number 3: Finally, is thy heart right with God before you get married? We read these words in Genesis 3:16; "I will greatly multiply your pain in childbirth..." You see these words tell us something about what was going on long before the "fall," and long after Adam and Eve were married. **What we must realize in this statement is that something cannot be multiplied unless something is already there.** In other words, if Eve never knew pain in childbirth, how then can zero pain be multiplied greatly? Pain in Eve existed prior to God multiplying her pain, which could mean she had prior births. For if Eve was sinless, why then the multiplied pain? We read in Revelation that a perfect state of sinlessness has no pain; "He will wipe away every tear from their eyes and death shall be no more, neither shall there be mourning nor crying no pain anymore..." Why then the pain, lest there be sin prior to the multiplied pain? You see, the sin is not the marriage, *it is the sinful souls in the marriage.* People who marry, bring to the marriage their own brand of sin. They bring their own pains to the marriage and the marriage in turn will multiply the pain they bring to the marriage. Many live in denial of their sins of the past. But the question we all must face before going into any relationship; "Is thy heart right with God...?"

Was Adam and Eve's heart right with God when God clearly stated to them that they were not to eat of the tree of the "knowledge of good and of evil?" Was Eve's heart right with her husband when she gave him of the fruit to eat before consulting with him? Was her heart right with God for blaming the serpent for her own deliberate act to disobey God? Was Adam's heart right with Eve and with God when he blamed God for giving Eve to him and then blamed Eve for his disobedience to God? What needs to be considered;

Is thy heart right with God before you marry,
and
Is thy heart right with God during your marriage?

June, 1996

Chapter Seven

THE 23RD PSALM

Psalm 23

In one of the more original forms of the 23rd Psalm, or at least a "fresh translation," according to B.W. Anderson's book, <u>Out Of The Depths</u>, this Psalm placed focus on Trust, Comfort and Protection. It addressed the needs of the ancient pastoralist. For instance, a version of this "fresh translation" reads as follows:

> "Yahweh is my Shepherd, nothing do I lack.
> In grassy meadows he makes me repose,
> By quiet waters he leads me.
> He revives my whole being!
> He guides me into the right paths, for the
> honor of His Name.
>
> Even when I go through the valley of deep darkness,
> I fear nothing sinister;
> For You are at my side!
> Your rod and staff reassure me.
>
> You spread out before me a table,
> In sight of those who threaten me.
> You pour upon my head festive oil
> My cup is brimming over!
>
> Certainly, divine goodness and grace attend me
> throughout all my days,
> And I shall be a guest in Yahweh's house
> as long as I live."[1]

This *fresh* version addresses the needs of shepherds and

---

1 Anderson, Bernhard W., <u>Out of the Depths</u>, pp. 144-145.

nomads living in a desert – a place where one is constantly surrounded by the perils of heat, wild beast, lack of water, killers and thieves. However, in comparing this version with that of an English translation of today, there is an irony which appears to be one of perception. For instance, in this version one finds that there is a total reliance on God for comfort, assurance and full protection from the dangers of the desert. On the other hand, in reading a more familiar version in today's English translations, these same characteristics are found to exist much in the choices made by the individual than on total reliance on God who supplies our every need. I suppose that the reason behind this line of thinking is because we, in our western culture, prize ourselves as being independent individualists capable of doing our own thing as opposed to eastern cultures which are more group dependency oriented.

For example, a line comparison between the two versions would read, "Yahweh is my Shepherd, nothing do I lack…" (Anderson's "fresh translation"). Today this expression would be, "The Lord is my Shepherd, I shall not want…" The difference, notably, between the two versions is found in the words 'lack' and 'want.' Put more plainly, a 'lack' more often than not denotes a need while 'want' more than likely denotes a choice.

Needs are normally associated with things germane to survival while wants are mostly associated with personal choices. The above current day English translation, "The Lord is my Shepherd, I shall not want," borders more closely on the edge of personal choice than on the need for total dependence on God. That God supplies our every need is not immediately apparent. Rather, it would appear that God is our Shepherd for the expressed purpose of supplying the desires of our hearts. On the other hand, the *fresh* version "Yahweh is my Shepherd, nothing do I lack," is a very strong statement giving God all the praise and credit for His continuous graces and mercies being poured out upon us, even with the drawing of our every breath. This version makes one constantly aware of their every need being supplied by God. They do not take God's graces and mercies for granted – even to the extent of being conscious of the fact that God supplies their every breath and heartbeat. Hence, in the *fresh* version, one readily recognizes that they are totally dependent upon God and the recognition of this fact is regularly reflected in one's use of language when speaking of God. It is a language inclusive of total dependence on God.

Further examples of line comparisons are as follows:
The *fresh* version would be, "He guides me into the right paths, for the honor of His Name..." While today's versions would read, "He leads me in the path of righteousness, for His namesake..."

Here again is a difference of perception. The phrase, right paths as compared with the phrase paths of righteousness, creates tension in my mind. For the former suggests a subordinate in need of direction while the latter suggests that one is by definition of their own worth, worthy of the righteousness of God. Furthermore, "for the honor of His Name" suggests an action originated by God for God's own sake while "for His namesake" though meaning the same, may also imply that the individual is doing God a favor. In other words, I'm going to do God a favor by letting him guide me in the path of righteousness, so I will not discredit his name.

Again, the *fresh* version would read, "Certainly, divine goodness and grace attend me throughout all my days..."

And today's version would read, "Surely, goodness and mercy shall follow me all the days of my life…"

Personal perception rules again in that "attend me" suggests that the writer of this Psalm recognizes constantly that it is in fact God's goodness and mercies that keep him from being caught-up in harm's way while "shall follow me" suggests that grace and mercy should, in fact, follow one around because of one's own individual goodness.

Hence, we must become more aware of how we understand the 23rd Psalm. We must understand it in light of how God freely extends His own goodness and mercies, and not because of how we define our own self-worth.

Furthermore, ancient pastoral people perceived God as the Good Shepherd who was Protector and Hospitable Host in a hostile environment. For as the sheep is led "in grassy meadows…by quiet waters," safely through the perils of the desert by the Shepherd, to the psalmist, God guides his footsteps through life, safely through the VALLEY OF THE SHADOW OF DEATH. In both instances, God is Protector. For a weary traveler in the midst of his desert enemies, amidst those who would kill and rob him while on his lonesome and dangerous journey, there is an unspoken law of hospitality, which rules the lives of desert dwellers. It is a law, which guarantees any traveler immunity from the bandits of the desert. The weary traveler is given food, shelter and comfort in the tent of another. He finds assurance in the tents of desert dwellers. Thus, the Psalmist also sees God as a host par-excellence. A host who spreads out before a weary traveler a welcome table of comfort and protection from those who would threaten him.

Therefore, this *fresh* version is a fitting Psalm for a pastoral people, shepherds in the deserts of Palestine who must make their living in a dangerous and deadly environment.

But today, we are not a pastoral people. Rather, we are products of job downsizing and job abolishment. We are products of the computer age, high-tech industrialist single-parent home, Affirmative Action, paycheck earning 8-5 Monday-Friday, dues-paying-go-to-church-on Sunday, people. We are filled with a life of stress, frustration, broken-homes, broken relationship, broken fellowship with other church members, smoking, drinking, social sipping and every now and then fun nipping, drug culture, neighborhood gangs, status seeking, upward mobile, competitive, people.

We are religious. We are Baptist, Methodist, Holiness, Islamic, Pentecostal tongue speaking and some tongues you don't want to hear speaking people who submerge ourselves in water to wash away our sins or immerge in alcohol to drown them type people.

Therefore, in light of this Psalm, how does this Psalm work for us today? How does this Psalm usher us through our Valley Of The Shadow Of Death in this 21st Century? For this Psalm must do for us today what it did for ancient Israel, and that is to put us in touch with God. We must today realize the many ways God provides for us as He did for the shepherds of old.

First, we must realize that when sheep are domesticated they lose something of their natural sense of survival and thus the shepherd must be there to supply their every need. Like sheep ourselves, we have become so hi-tech, that we in turn have lost something of who it is that supplies our every need. It's not our jobs, our own abilities, nor the conveniences at our fingertips in this electronic/computer age, but it is God.

Secondly, we must regain the realization of how totally dependent we are on God as sheep are on the shepherd of the flock. As the shepherds feed their sheep in green pasture, we must be fed the word of God less we die in our sins. As the shepherd waters his sheep, we must be watered with the baptism of the Holy Spirit so as not to drown in our sins. We must realize as written in the lyrics of an old Gospel tune:

I need the Lord to guide me everyday, as I travel along this narrow way.
Though afflictions oppress my soul, I'm determine to reach my goal;
for I've got to have Jesus for I just can't make it by myself.

Yet, before we can begin to understand how this Psalm works for us today, we must come to understand something about our perceptions. Perceptions play a tremendous role in how we understand our experiences and what we read.

To demonstrate a misunderstood perception, the story is told of a young soldier returning to post on a train routed through a very dark tunnel. On this train with him sitting opposite each other was a general, a young attractive girl and an elderly lady. Mid-way through this tunnel there was the sound of a kiss and a slap. The general, young girl and the elderly lady all thought the sound and effect were the result of a misplaced flirtatious kiss and a retaliatory slap. However, in truth it was none of the above; rather, the young soldier enjoyed the opportunity of telling other soldiers on post how much fun it was to kiss the back of his hand and slap a general without getting a court martial.

Hence, the way in which we come to understand how this Psalm works for us today largely depends on our perceptions. We must understand it in light of the ancient shepherds of old in that God is a God who supplies our every need. It is with this understanding that we can continue to read this psalm in new light.

Again the phrase, "He restores my soul" gives way to the *fresh* version, "He revives my whole being." For the verb restores which simply means to "put back into a former state," needs the added ingredient of the verb revives which means awaken to consciousness. For to be restored to our former state might not be a great improvement over the prior stressful and abnormal state in which we once existed. What is needed is an awakening. Restoration without revival does not promise spiritual renewal. But in the *fresh* version, the psalmist adds the missing ingredient of revival; "...a new and right spirit within..." When one is revived, they come alive because the word of God lives in them. This living word is what causes us to immediately retreat from the current evil we are practicing. God's word awakens us to a higher level of conscious awareness of Him, which opens our understanding and brightens up our daily living because, "Thy *Word O Lord Is A Lamp Unto My Feet And A Light Unto My Path*" (Psalms).

Finally, in today's translation, "He leads me in the path of righteousness..." may send mixed signals to the minds of some, if compared with the *fresh* version, "He guides me into the right path." The today's translation may tend to make one feel they have earned the right to be led by God, "in the path of righteousness," as though they deserve to be led by God in no other path but righteousness. But, in the *fresh* version, one is submissive to the guiding hand of the Lord for it is the Lord who "guides me [us] into the right path," less we choose the wrong path every time. The power is given to God to guide us in the "right path" and we must appreciate God's guidance. We must not claim the righteous path for ourselves, rather we are led by God "in the path of righteousness."

Righteousness is of God, not that we ourselves are deserving of it. Hence, in the midst of our undeserving existence, we hear the words of encouragement in song and need to remain mindful;

> *I need the Lord to guide me every day,*
> *as I travel along life's narrow way.*
> *Tho' afflictions oppress my soul,*
> *I'm determine to reach my goal.*
> *For I've got to have Jesus*
> *for I just can't make it by myself.*

July 23, 1995

Chapter Eight

TO BE RAISED AND RESURRECTED

Ezekiel 37: 1-14
(With Special Emphasis on 1, 5, 10)

These verses might suggest to one what it means to be alive but dead, raised but not resurrected. Ezekiel observed that the exiled nation of Israel had been reduced to dry bones as a result of their spiritual amputation from God – and then raised by the power of God to become an, "exceedingly great army."

However, the vision of Ezekiel is not about a vision of death and resurrection but rather is a kind of vision of a life form for which one is bodily alive but consciously dead. This is not a kind of 'personal guilt-tripping' consciousness where one can shut themselves off from their guilt rather than face it, but conscious unawareness of their surroundings. His was a vision of dead-living beings. This sea of dead-living souls, a sea of raised bodies and non-resurrected minds, was for Ezekiel a perplexing sight. How could one be alive and dead at the same time?

We know that life presents us with many perplexing problems while being perplexing itself. Life is a mystery! It is a mystery not at all easy to understand. Often in our living, we find life is caught-up in a space between the conscious and the unconscious, positioned in such ways as to keep the two separate rather than being a bridge between them. Ezekiel saw this unusual existence of life. He saw bones raised, yet they were void of consciousness and speech. Ezekiel was seeing a kind of life form that had no conscious awareness. In other words, what he saw was a sea of dead-living beings – life without spirit, without consciousness, life in limbo.

But this kind of life form is not surprising. For the concept of dead-living is not new to the human experience; neither is it foreign to the Bible. For time and again the writers of the Bible record how absence from the spirit of God is death, not a bodily death, but a kind of conscious and spiritual death. Isaiah wrote in 59:1,2, that our iniquities separate us from God, (i.e., when our awareness and consciousness levels of conditions about us are at lowest ebb) and that God hides his face from us, ultimately resulting in the dead, living.

Paul's advice to Timothy on this same matter of dead-living concerned the life of widows. Paul said of those widows who prefer a life of pleasure to a life of supplication and prayer constitutes a form of dead-living. Paul wrote in his letter to Timothy, "she that is alive in pleasure is dead while she lives" (1Tim.5:16). But Jesus says it best, "Follow me... and let the dead bury their own dead," (Luke 9:59,60).

Thus, we see that the non-resurrected mind is dead-living, a form of spiritual death which Ezekiel saw. Earlier the Israelites had testified of themselves that, "our bones are dried up, and our hope is lost; we are cut off completely" (11). Thus, Ezekiel saw Isaiah's prophecy come true.

Ezekiel saw the nation of Israel in a state of mental stupor. Israel was scattered, confused, divided, unmotivated, and unconcerned. Israel was without leadership, purposeless, powerless, exploitable and left as a nation of waste. All this and more became for Ezekiel a symbol of Israel's dry bones. Israel was spiritually dead – apart from God. She had become a nation of dead-living beings, a valley of dry bones – raised but not resurrected.

But there is a message for us today to be learned from Ezekiel's vision. It is a simple but important message. It is a message that shows and warns us what happens to a people who are spiritually dead (living apart from God). For the message suggests irrevocably that, "without the Spirit of God" no matter how one looks, dresses or how wealthy and powerful, he is still dead without God. It is a simple message that also speaks to people about the difference between just living in the community and of being alive and doing something about the degrading conditions in the communities they are a part of.

In a sense, spiritual death can affect a person, a community or a nation. It can even affect the church. Spiritual death attacks and kills not the body but the mind. Life can continue in the body as Ezekiel observed, but not the mind. It takes something special other than flesh and bones to give life to the mind. Someone said that the mind is a terrible thing to lose...and the implication of that statement is directed towards the conditions of black America. And I am concerned about that, on resurrection morning. For a look at our black communities of today, is a grim testimony to all of black America that our concept of the resurrection of Jesus from Joseph's tomb is not much different from Jesus' painful experience of being crucified on the cross of Calvary.

In other words, if our concept of Jesus' resurrection is one of producing a new life in Christ, then all of our present worshipping and beliefs in Christ have not produced conditions in the black community equitable to our beliefs and practices of what the resurrection means. For the painful conditions that still exist in the black communities of today is more akin to the painful experience of Jesus' crucifixion as opposed to His glorious resurrection from

145

the pain of the cross. For one needs only to look at the black communities of America to discover this. And I am not talking about our communities being deprived of substances, but rather being deprived of a sense of unity; a sense of community unity and spiritual awakening.

Again if Jesus' resurrection symbolizes for us, liberation from suffering, oppression and ignorance, then I have a grim story to share with you this celebrated resurrection morning. It is a story for which suffering, oppression and ignorance are still cataclysmic in the black communities of America because of community disunity and a lack of spiritual awakening.

For the story of Jesus' life, death and resurrection is much more than a religious exercise on Easter morning. Resurrection is about a change, not an exercise in religious interpretations and religious concepts for Easter services. It's about a change of heart that brings about a change of conditions. A songwriter said it like this:

> *"What A Wonderful Change In My Life Has Been*
> *Wrought*
> *Since Jesus Came Into My Heart.*
> *I Have Light In My Soul For Which*
> *Long I Had Sought...*
> *Since Jesus Came Into My Heart.."*

Yet something is wrong in terms of how we have come to understand this change. For when we look at ourselves, about 35 million plus strong, we come up with some startling similarities with those people who were found in the valley of dry bones. We are rapidly becoming a nation of dead-living souls, alive in the body – dead in the spirit. A raised people but not resurrected. For instance, although we have many admirable characteristics, we are still dangerously lacking in too many areas of spiritual unity and community accountability.

For instance, in 1974 the money flow in the black communities of America was $60 billion; in 1980, it rose to $126 billion; in 1982, $155 billion; a projection for 1984, $200 billion. A future projection at this rate for the 90's will be over $450 billion. This flow of money in the black community works out to this: That of the 158 nations in the world today, if black people in America were counted as a nation, it would mean that in 1980, we ranked in the 13th position from the top, in terms of money flow and wealth. Beyond 1982, we rose to occupy the sixth position and beyond.

Now this is not black economic poverty, rather this is black mal-distribution of prosperity. It is a displacement of priorities and values. We find ourselves alive in a living space of not knowing where to begin to pull ourselves together to act as a united force in the fight against black economic conditions of powerlessness. For example, the irony of it all is that this money did not go towards community improvements, it did not address the needs of the suffering masses, but rather went towards personal care products, and personal uses. This kind of money was spent on travel, junk food, soft drinks, alcoholic beverages, recreations, entertainment, clothing, and household furnishings. *In other words, we've got it – we don't know how to use it, share it, or invest it*.

For example, during the year of 1980, the purchase pattern of middle income black families as compared to the total purchase pattern of the USA looked like this: We drank 44% of all the soft drinks consumed in America, and of all the cigarettes smoked in America we smoked 45% of them.

We ate 32% of all the canned ham in America, and we used 81% of all the shortening. Of all the bourbon whiskey, we consumed 17%; 18% of all the scotch whiskey, and 27% of all the rum. Blacks spent over 360 million dollars alone on champagne, cold duck, and wine. We ate over 30 million dollars in potato chips. And of the total number of fur and fancy fur stoles sold in America in 1980, black women purchased one-half of them. Black women bought 74% of all cosmetics sold in America and of perfumes and colognes sold to the American public, black women bought 91%.

If we look at ourselves from an educational stand-point-of-view, black people are viewed as having a population in 1980 of 25 million plus. Of the 12 million blacks 25 and older, 6 million never finished high school. Of the 231,203 black owned firms and businesses of all sorts, except the black church, only 1,834 were dedicated to the education of 25 million plus people. Of the multitude of black social problems we have in America; i.e., education, welfare, economical exploitation, poverty, sickness, mental illnesses, domestic problems, drugs, dope and everything else, there were only 810 black owned firms dedicated to the care of these problems. Now when we combine these problems with mis-management and mis-directed funds, confusion of priorities and ignorance, and put them against the backdrop of 60,000 plus black churches, 15 million plus black church members and 55,000 plus black pastors – with these conditions still existing, we can only draw one conclusion, that we as a church and a nation of black people need to be resurrected.

But our hope is not lost, for resurrection comes when we are able to defeat those things most debasing to us. It comes when we can take a soul off welfare, save a mind from being wasted and teach a whole community about a man named Jesus who came to set at liberty those who are oppressed, who lived, died and arose for that purpose. And when we can begin to become accountable to our communities, then we can sing with new meaning and sincerity;

"I am possessed of a hope that is steadfast and sure
since Jesus came into my heart.
And no dark clouds of doubt now my pathway
to obscure
since Jesus came into my heart."

April 3, 1983

Chapter Nine

DEACONS

Acts 6:1-10, Romans 16:1-2

Deacon, in its simplest form, means servant, attendant, minister. It is also used as a title given to a select group of people who by the church has been charged with performing the special task of keeping peace and harmony in the church. Aside from the office of the preachers and the choir members the office of the deacon is the third most major, oldest and respected office in the Christian Church.

The respect we attribute to the diaconate order, is not only because it is an ancient order of the church or that it has survived as long as the church...but rather because of the service for which it is suppose to give. In other words, the word used in Acts about deacons, (the Greek word *diaconos)* is a word that describes what a deacon does in work and in service. It is not a title! Yet, deacon conveys another meaning. It carries the meaning that these are trained men and women who are active in the business of serving those in need. But, aside from this description we need to look briefly at four other areas of a deacon:

a) Their rank in the church
b) Duties of a deacon
c) Historical beginning of the diaconate order
d) Characteristic traits of a deacon

Their Rank
First, we know that they <u>ranked</u> third after bishops and elders, in the ordained ministry. The deacon was distinctly the bishop's assistant, being ordained by the bishop alone

and serving him in his church and pastoral duties. At one time the deacons received the offerings of the people and administered the elements of Communion. At a later time in the church, they not only received the offerings and administered the elements, but also had the exclusive right of reading the gospel lectern at the service of the Lord's Supper.

They also sought out and visited the sick, the poor and indigent – especially widows and orphans and prisoners; informed the bishop of the needs of the misfortunate ones and carried to the poor the alms of the church. (Now another order of the deacons was the *deaconesses*.) The office of the deaconess was none the less important. Although the New Testament does not give us clear indications of the ministerial order of the deaconess, there are certainly clear indications in the New Testament that this order does exist! (Romans 16:1, Philippians 1:1).

Their Duties
It is commonly assumed that deaconesses do have specific functions in the church and that at least two of these functions can be traced back as far as about 300 AD, during the days of Constantine. These functions were: To assist at the baptism of women and also the anointing of;

a) women to special callings,
b) to go into the houses of the heathen where there were women,
c) to visit with those who were sick, to minister to those in need and
d) to bathe those women who had started to recover from their illnesses.

However, for the diaconate orders, in light of their duties and because they will be in contact constantly with the general public, exposed to a host of temptations and be responsible for the church's material offerings, his or her character must be impeccable! For many temptations are open to the diaconate order for gossip, slander and intemperance.

Thus, Paul would write that they are to be of good repute, full of the Spirit and of wisdom. Stephen, a man full of faith and of the Holy Spirit, sets the best example for the office of the diaconate to follow.

Historical Beginning
The diaconate began with the selection and ordination of *seven* whose job it was to assist the twelve in the distributions of charitable provisions to the local widows. Now these twelve, were no doubt Apostles of Christ who were trained to preach, teach and carry on the gospel labors of Jesus. They were in essence Evangelists. They were divinely chosen for the specific task of preaching and extending the work of Christ.

These twelve concerned themselves with the spiritual needs of the people, making it their business to deal specifically with those things divine and heavenly. They were not church administrators, rulers of the people, nor community leaders. They were not church appointed officials, neither were they taught by an ecclesiastical body. Their task primarily was to get on with the business of preaching and teaching the gospel and not become tied down in the mechanics and details of the problems which befalls the church community.

But, as it happened, a problem arose in the early church that was so great it affected their preaching and teaching ministry. The problem was the widows of the Christian Greeks were being neglected in the daily distribution of charities. It seemed as though the Christian Jewish widows were getting all the charities while the Christian Greeks were not. Parts of the church community were being neglected. This created a split in the church; confusion arose. Hostilities and jealousies were so thick as to disturb the morning services (if I may use that analogy). No one could keep their mind on the preaching amidst this spiritual chaos. Dishevelment and disorder ruled the worship services so much that preaching became increasingly difficult if not impossible at times.

At one point, the twelve may have thought about giving up preaching because of the massive confusion in the church. Either that or at least they must have felt that they could no longer preach effectively until something was done about the confusion. But at any rate, we know that they had to stop their preaching and deal with the problem. For in Acts we read that the twelve (apostles) summoned the body of the disciples (church) and said, "It is not right that we should neglect the word of God to wait on tables" (Acts 6:2). For to serve tables involved many things. The poor had to be fed, the widows taken care of, clothing and monies had to be distributed and recorded, and order had to be maintained. It involved work! It involved good administration! It involved methods of caring for the poor and the widows! It involved handing out fair shares of provisions for those in need and keeping records of the distributions made.

Thus, it became necessary for the twelve to appoint servants to tend to the serving of tables. It was, therefore, the job of these seven deacons to tend the needy, thereby freeing the Apostles to preach the word of God.

Yet, there was another role the deacons played. And this

was one of bridging the gap between feuding groups in the church. It was the deacons' task to act as a mediator and to also act to settle the bickering within groups so that harmony might be maintained in the church.

Hence, the church then with its problems of trying to bridge gaps between group factions, did not differ from the church of today. For example, the problems of the church today are three:

1. First the church body is enslaved to a network of church traditions.
2. The church body is stagnated today and will not grow simply because untrained, uninformed and often unsaved people occupy the position of leadership in the church.
3. There are too many people in the church who nurse petty differences and old grudges. Hence, included in the church body is all of the above.

Therefore, evangelism should begin in the congregation.

Yet, a major problem in the church of today is one of unresolved petty differences. Because of these differences, our churches are torn asunder. For the churches that are not literally torn apart, there is an unpleasant and unhealthy spirit of dissension that pervade the worshipping atmosphere. People learn to harbor old hostilities and petty grudges. Too often small differences go unresolved for too long only to develop later into unsolvable problems, then the church splits, physically, spiritually or both.

But many of these differences and attitudes come about as a result of the church having become something other than what it should be. For instance, the church as it is supposed to be, is a church that houses the free spirit of God. With this spirit of freedom, it therefore, becomes the mission of the church to free its people from the shackles of ignorance. Thus, the church is supposed to give us a religion that is free and open to the revelations of God and a freedom to express these revelations. The church is, therefore, supposed to be a mission of freedom and not a mission contrary to freedom. It is to be a missionary church for giving freedom and not a mission contrary to the freedom of the church. The church must be free!

But what we see today is the church in competition. Churches in traditional competition with one another competing for the largest congregations and the best singing choirs. Today's church is a church that is bound by the customs of building beautiful buildings, while caught-up in the traditions of ostentatious church worship. Emphasis is on how beautiful your worship service was in your beautiful church this morning, as opposed to how beautiful your services were to the needy in the community last week.

Thus, we see the church of today, too bound up in traditions and not grounded enough in revelations and freedom. All of these religiosities and churchly attitudes, join to strip the church of its original mission to spiritually serve the people and "to set at liberty those who are oppressed." Yet, these churchly attitudes come by means of how we understand the church of today. For we speak of the church being in us; but in reality what we are experiencing is a church built by us and we are in the building. Because of this, we come to understand the church as a building which houses our religious beliefs and practices, rather than a place where God is continuously revealing His will to us.

In other words, a religion that is housed in a building gives rise to its own set of unique religious problems. For in a building, we have problems that are relative to the building simply because our understanding of religion is in association with the building we worship in, rather than understanding that the symbolism behind the rending of the veil in the temple is the end of the church institutionalized and the beginning of the church becoming involved in community needs. This is not too difficult to understand. For if we consider the problems we are faced with in our religion, we will find them to be relative to the building than that of the community. For instance, in the building, we scold about not bringing our Bibles to church, we complain about our church attendance falling off and our buildings falling apart from lack of repairs; and that we are not giving enough tithes and offerings to support the church's finances. Preaching becomes preaching of the above, as well as the preaching of the unresolved personal issues in the pastor's life. We are also faced with other church issues peculiar to the building, when we make statements like:

It's against church policy...
It won't work in our church...
We are not ready for that kind of change...
We had not better purchase that new item for it
might run up the overhead...

We even struggle with problems created by the choir, often called the 'war department' of the church.

Thus, we spend too much time wrestling with relevant things to the building and at the same time irrelevant to the spirit of the church in communion with community needs. The preaching of the gospel of Jesus is less that of the preaching of church issues. These things are just some of the problems of our 21st Century for which our deacons must train themselves to address.

Therefore, the diaconate order must be above reproach in order to address these problems. They must be of good repute, of unquestionable character, and be respected in church and community. They must be learned men and women, for they are charged with the awesome task of bringing hearts together in Christ. They must be filled with the Spirit and of wisdom. For if they have made a decision for Christ, then they must practice living the life of the decision they have made.

Finally, We Come To The Character Traits Of A Deacon
The scripture tells us that *seven* were picked. We know that the number seven alone has a sacred connotation. For it denotes completeness, fullness, unity and holiness. For whenever we see its use in the Bible, it is used as a kind of symbol that symbolizes spiritual totality: On the seventh day, God rested from His work of creation. God then blessed the seventh day. Naaman dipped in the Jordan River seven times to be cured of leprosy.

Forgiveness is measured in terms of seventy times seven. Isaiah records Seven Spirits of God. The walls of Jericho fell after seven Priests, with seven trumpets, marched around the walls of Jericho seven times in seven days, and on the seventh blast of the trumpets, the walls came tumbling down. Jesus had seven last words to say from the cross before He died.

Seven deacons, complete in the Spirit, not complete because they were seven in number, but implied in the number seven is a spiritual message, which says they belong to a spiritual body complete in Christ.

No longer are they caught between the church and the world undecided which way to turn. Their completeness in Christ is best expressed in the song, "I have decided to make Jesus my choice." These are men and women who have already come out of the wilderness into the marvelous light.

Thus, the seven deacons selected compose the complete character of what deacons are to be like:

Characteristics of a Deacon
1. Stephen - Crown. You see a deacon must be crowned with the Holy Spirit. Stephen was "a man full of faith and of the Holy Spirit." The first qualification of a deacon is that he or she must be full of the Holy Spirit and of *Faith*.

Faith is necessary in order to put down confusion in the church. A deacon who does not have faith in God, will get caught up in the problems of the church and take sides with friends or the stronger force, and instead of becoming a solution to the problem they become part of the problem. But a deacon with faith is something else. Faith will establish you on solid grounds with the Lord. Faith enables you to be your own man or woman in the Lord. Faith will cause you to love the saints and side with the right. By faith you can move that mountain of despair in the church. By faith Abraham obeyed the Lord and by faith deacons will do the same. Faith opens the doors of our hearts so that the Holy Spirit may enter. Then a deacon full of the Holy Spirit, heals the wounds of the church. They know how to get to the troubled spots in the church and every now and then when the saints of God are not setting well with one another, as saints ought, the deacons with the Holy Spirit will meet with them and say

I know there are some problems you cannot solve, but I
know also of somebody you can take your troubles to:

"Let us have a little talk with Jesus.
Tell Him all about your troubles
He will hear your faintest cry
And answer by and by. Then you will
Feel a little prayer wheel turning,
You will feel a little fire burning in your soul.
Having a little talk with Jesus makes things alright."

Somebody else said it this way:

"You can't hurry God you just have to wait,
You've got to trust and give Him time,
no matter how long it takes...

For He's a God you can't hurry
He'll be there, you need not worry.

He may not come when you want Him
but he is right on time."

You see a deacon must wear that crown, "full of faith
and the Holy Spirit." But that ain't all!...

2. Philip – Brotherhood. He was known as the
   Evangelist spreading the word of
   God everywhere he went. A deacon must be a
   brother to the saints of God. A
   deacon is a brother to the brotherless.
3. Prochorus (*Prok-ca-rus*). He administered relief to
   the widows, and relieved the oppressed from their
   sufferings. A deacon is a *comforter*.

4. Nicanor (*Ny-ka-nor*) – Conqueror. He administered relief to the poor, a conqueror of poverty. A deacon is a *conqueror of poverty*.
5. Timon (*Ty-mon*) – Honor is God. He assisted in the daily administration of relief to the needy Christians and engaged in the missionary work of the Lord. A deacon is *honorable*. They are missionaries of mercy.
6. Parmenas (*Par-menas*) – Steadfast. He ministered to the needy and kept on preaching 'keep the faith.' Have faith in God and He will see you through and every now and then, when you feel no one cares, the Lord has a mighty sweet way of sending someone around just to say hello, I was thinking about you today – thought I'd drop by to see how you are doing. A deacon is *steadfast in the faith*.
7. Nicolaus – Victory over the people. The one who ministered to the whole gamut of human miseries. From him a deacon *learns how to pray for everybody*.

Thus, from these seven we learn that deacons are caring men and women of God. For by their faith they have learned to walk with God.

O Master let me walk with thee
(is the theme of the deacon)
In lowly paths of service free: Tell me thy secret, help me bear,
The strain of toil, the fret of care.

And finally, it is the deacon's task to serve those in need. To sow the seeds of peace and harmony and pray for those in need. Then shall their song be:

163

"May the service I give speak for me,
when I've done the best
I can and my friends don't understand, may the service
I've given speak for me.
The work I've done, it seems so small
Sometimes it seems like nothing at all
But when I stand before my God
I want to hear Him say, Well done.
May the work I've done speak for me."

October 3, 1982

Chapter Ten

GOD DOES NOT WILL SUFFERING

Isaiah 61:1-2; Luke 4:16-21; Matt. 11:28-30; Matt.18:12-14; 2 Pet.3:8-9

To know something about the world of suffering and the attitudes of people toward suffering in the days of Isaiah and Jesus, is to know today that the 'event of suffering' in the world never changes. The attitudes of people toward suffering may change, but not the historical and political times that produce the events of suffering. Human suffering will always exist. From one generation to another, suffering will leave in its wake long lasting, painful effects; both physical and psychological. Suffering also leaves long lasting, negative attitudes in its wake. These attitudes are transmitted from generation to generation and will remain in place for generations yet unborn to inherit. Such trans-generational attitudes toward suffering tend to suggest that along with its long reaching effects, suffering is a divine will of God. But that is not so! For God "…is patient with you, not wanting anyone to perish…" (2 Pet.3:9); and that God's "yoke is easy." Thus, in light of these scriptures, *God does not will suffering.*

Now, in view of the above, we must remember that although the occurrences of human suffering do not change, people's attitudes toward suffering do change. For instance, the victims of suffering and the social and historical events of human suffering are not the same. The attitudes of suffering victims differ because their personal feelings and emotions are involved in their suffering experiences. Suffering is a part of living. We learn about it during any social and historical time period. Hence, those who learn about suffering from the academics of the time, stand at a distance from the personal experiences felt by the victims of those suffering times. Furthermore, the victims' attitudes toward suffering differ in bitterness and intensity from individual to individual, and from time period to time period.

But for the most part, to demonstrate the differences in the suffering victims' attitudes, we must look at two basic historical time periods. For instance, the attitudes of the victims involved in the suffering from slavery in the Old Testament are not the same as the attitudes of the suffering victims involved in the institution of slavery in America. The two events of human suffering do not change, but the intensity of the suffering victims' attitudes differ. What must be considered is, the historical time period produces the intensity of the suffering victims' attitudes. One needs only to read the two historical records of slavery to discover that the after-effects of slavery of Africans in America are by far quite different from the after-effects of slavery in the Old Testament. The reason for this rest on the nature and intensity of the suffering experience of the times. The magnitude of the bitter experiences of the slaves seems to be in proportion to the endurance and intensity of the lingering bitter attitudes of the victims. Simply put, suffering of any magnitude is no stranger to humanity and no amount of suffering is welcome in the human experience. But types and tolerances to suffering are unique to the historical period. Each historical period produces its own unique brand of bitter attitudes towards suffering in the hearts of the victims. Hence, the human experience of suffering in each historical time period appears as though suffering is a divine will. Yet, a closer look at human suffering clearly reveals that God does not will suffering, neither is suffering a divine will of God.

But, be it the sufferings of biblical times, today suffering is a daily occurrence the world over. Suffering is so much a part of the human experience that many will look to their religious beliefs in order to justify suffering as being a normal condition of the human experience. For this reason, I suppose suffering would become more acceptable if it could be divinely justified as being a normal condition of God's will and character. But such a view on universal suffering raises the possibility that suffering must therefore, be a divine will of God because it happens to all. Yet if this is the case, then suffering can be reasoned from the position that it is a normal condition of the human family, thus it is divinely willed by God. What would follow is irrational deductive reasoning and wrong religious interpretations to support the false idea of the *normalcy of universal human suffering*. For if universal suffering is normal for the human family then it can be further deduced that suffering, in fact, has divine sanction. But we need to further investigate two propositions on the views of the normalcy of universal human suffering.

First, in Romans 8:28, we read, "…all things work together for good to them that love God, to them who are the called according to *his* purpose…" (KJV). Although suffering is not mentioned in this scripture, it can be easily implied. One must be careful in reading a negative implication into this scripture. It does not say that inclusive in "all things" one must suffer consistently to do the will of God or that suffering is a prerequisite to redemption. What must be seen in this scripture is not the necessary bitterness of suffering but rather a starting point of liberating people from suffering, not plunging them into it. For in the opening phrase "…all things work together for good…" implies both suffering and liberation from suffering. However, what is key to this scripture is the divine actions of God liberating us from suffering because the nature of God is good. In other words, we may suffer but we are not Divinely willed to suffer. As Dr. King once said, "unearned suffering is redemptive" but not a necessary condition of the human experience.

Secondly, we need to discuss further that one might have to suffer in order to complete a task and that sometimes suffering is non-preventable. But non-preventable suffering is not a doctrine carved in stone. Enoch and Elijah can attest to that. For one does not have to suffer in order to be redeemed because suffering is not a guarantee for redemption. Not only that but suffering for a task does not imply universal suffering as being normal for the human family. But, to hear the sum of it all, it takes the in-breaking event of the Kingdom of God into the human experience to show us that suffering is not a part of God's divine will. Revelation and inspiration teaches us this. Also, our Lord Jesus Christ teaches us to "seek first the Kingdom of God and His righteous…" In both instances nothing about universal suffering is implied, rather in both instances what is offered is a way out of suffering and a key to universal salvation.

Therefore, we would be wrong to include human suffering as one of the necessary human events implied in the Romans' scripture "all things." For with that kind of reasoning, we suggest to ourselves and to others that God is a God of violence and injustice. This is not true! **God does not will suffering.** His desire is that we should repent and turn to Him and live. For He is a God who "…have no pleasure in the death of anyone,…"(Ezekiel 18:32).

We must now turn to observe the primary activities of God in the human experience, which are ridding humanity of suffering. For the Bible reveals that the basic character of

God is one of freeing us from suffering. He is the one who in turn makes liberation from any form of bondage and suffering His primary concern. God relieves from suffering; "...The Spirit of the Lord is upon me because he has anointed me to bring good news to the poor..." (Luke 4:18-19).

Suffering, therefore, is not a condition of God's will, neither were we created to suffer. Because of this divine fact, we need to look more specifically at the belief that suffering is a condition of the human experience because it comes as a result of our disobedience to God. A contrasting example of human suffering, as a result of our disobedience to God and that of God's character of suffering not being a part of His divine will, is found in Genesis 15ff. We find in the story of Abraham, God's desire to keep us free from suffering. As the scriptures record, Abraham did not go into bondage to suffer the taskmaster's whip. Rather, Abraham "went to his ancestors in peace...(and was)...buried in a good old age" (15). He did not violate God's will, it was his descendants who did. They were the ones who suffered 430 years of bondage.

Yet, God never changes from His nature of being good. God relieves suffering. For in spite of the fact that Abraham's descendants violated God's will, whom God called a "stiff-neck people," God still remained true to His basic nature of righteousness, goodness, freedom, mercy and grace. For in the same instance where God was foretelling Abraham that his descendants would be slaves and oppressed for over 400 years, God also told him, "...I will bring judgment on the nation which enslaved them and afterwards they shall come out..." (14).

Simply said, we realize that suffering is a real condition in humanity, but it is not a real part of God's divine will. What God saw in His creation, which is also a reflection of His perfect image and character, is recorded in Genesis 1:31, "...everything that he had made...indeed...was very good."

Thus, when we see suffering in the scripture, we also see God moving to relieve us from suffering. In Ezekiel, we find that suffering was a common occurrence in Israel's community, so much so, that both spiritual and political leader would naturally practice oppressing their own people. But whenever suffering, oppression and injustice polluted the land so much, it was at that point God intervened and commanded, "And my princes shall no longer oppress my people... Enough, O princes of Israel! Put away violence and oppression and do what is just and right" (45:8,9).

Again, it was only 150 years prior to Ezekiel when Isaiah was struggling with the same problem of human suffering. We read about God's dissatisfaction being voiced against those who were contributors to human suffering. According to God, anyone wanting to work in His service had to first relieve the suffering of the people by means of: "...loosing the bonds of the wicked, undoing the throngs of the yoke and letting the oppressed go free." Furthermore, they had to "...break every yoke...and share their bread with the hungry and to bring the homeless poor into their own houses..." (58:6,7).

Yet, we find that human suffering is so widespread that too often we assume it has Divine justification. A look at today's global suffering is enough to boggle our minds. It will even confuse our religious perception into believing that suffering must be the will of God because it would appear that we are too helpless to do anything about it. Approximately one-fourth of the world's population fall under the definition of some form of human suffering. Yet, God is not the source of the problem, rather He is on the side of the solution. Jesus made that clear in Luke when He spoke in the synagogue one Sabbath, "The Spirit of the Lord is upon me...because He has anointed me to set at liberty those who are oppressed." (4:18f).

What, therefore, must be considered is the way people live and treat one another; be it in the world, community, church or home. The way we treat one another has a lot to do with creating conditions, which prevail to produce widespread suffering. Well over 500 million people in the world face starvation everyday. Added to this are wars, high-tech weapons and weapons of mass destruction. One nuclear submarine has enough nuclear firepower, if unleashed, to annihilate all life forms on the earth.

Such becomes an attack upon God's creation. I am convinced that should such an unleashing of such mass destruction ever occur, God would not stand-by impartial to the senseless and insane destruction of His creation. His response would be a swift and absolute intervention. Sodom and Gomorrah, along with the flood in Noah's days, are demonstrative of the intervening power of God. God knows how to protect His own.

Yet, in the midst of these perplexities, stands the God of Justice and Righteousness. God acts to remove suffering: *To the writer of Exodus*, God exclaims, "I have seen the afflictions of my people...I know their suffering and I have come down to deliver them." *To the Chronicles*, God demands "If my people...will seek My face and turn from their wicked ways, then I will...forgive their sin and heal

173

their land." *To Isaiah*, God commands "...break every yoke. *To Ezekiel*, God commands "Enough." *To Luke*, God came in the person of Jesus "...to set at liberty those who are oppressed." "Come unto me," said Jesus, "all you that labor and are heavy laden and I will give you rest...for My yoke is easy and My burden is light." For a Righteous God is about the business of relieving suffering.

God in times past as even today, hates oppression and human suffering. For the position God takes against any form of human suffering and oppression is stated by Him in Ezekiel 18:32. And God's character does not change from generation to generation when it comes to relieving human suffering. For to the victim as well as the oppressor, God said to both, "turn to me and live, for I have no pleasure in the death of anyone." Is not, therefore, *the essence of God his goodness? God does not will suffering.* His will is that we be made whole in Him, see how His eternal goodness is captured in this song:

Come Ye disconsolate, wherever you languish.
Come to the mercy seat, fervently kneel.
Here bring your wounded heart, here tell your anguish.
Earth has no sorrow, heaven cannot heal!

January, 1982

Chapter Eleven

BLACK RELIGIOUS DIGNITY AND THE GOSPEL

Deuteronomy 4:32-33, 35; St. Luke 4:16-19

American Christianity has not done much since 1787, to tumble the walls of religious separation between the black and white churches in America. And maybe because racial segregation is so characteristic of the American system, more and more black people are beginning to wonder about the validity and type of Christianity flowing from our American churches. This suspicion seems to be focused on whether the practices of the religion of Christianity in the American churches, are in fact biblical Christianity or just another lifestyle of the total American way of segregation which spills over into the American system of religions.

However, this ancient church-related racial split has caused many blacks to realize with greater intensity the need to know more about their heritage. That this 'snowballing' urge to 'hop on the bandwagon' of the black experience is in some way related to our encounters with American Christianity and the meeting of the American Christ. We know there is a significant and distinct difference between the practices of American Christianity and that of the Christianity of Jesus in the Bible. We also know that this difference accounts largely for the reasons why many black people want to know more about their longtime hidden American heritage. Many black people have learned that Black Power, black nationalism and black theology, their history, heritage, and black culture are really nothing to be apprehensive about – nor are they sacrilegious. Furthermore, many have discovered that these experiences are identical themes with those of the gospel. For in the studies of the black experiences in America, one finds that there is a unified theme of liberating poor people from oppression, which flow the same throughout the gospel of Jesus Christ.

However, the coming of black awareness is not without its problems for it raises serious issues in the religious lives of many; especially black people. For instance, the black experience questions and answers many of the conditions of black people. This black experience deals directly with many of the unsolved problems and issues of blacks. How black is Jesus and all of the other biblical characters we are so accustomed to singing and praying about? How black are these biblical people, especially when we read the Bible and find similarity of their struggles with those of blacks in America? Is there any relationship between the liberation of poor people from oppression and the blackness of Jesus; if so, is it significant to our religious practices? Having said this, are there in the annals of the human experience a kinship between color and conditions? Do experiences of the Jews in the Bible represent their condition as a result of their color (blackness), as do experiences of blacks in America represent our conditions as a result of our color (blackness)?

Thus, in light of the issues raised, black theology – which is an offspring of the black experience – seeks to find answers. Not only does it seek to find the answers to the blackness of Jesus, but how His blackness ties in with the whole theme of liberating people from oppression and ignorance, in accordance with Jesus' preaching of the gospel. For example, when black people are asked about the importance of the blackness of Jesus and they respond in a bewildered and amazed tone as if to say *whatever difference does His color make in terms of my salvation* – then this response becomes the whole issue. Black theology seeks to investigate why the issue of the blackness of Jesus triggers an unfavorable emotional response in black people and yet they will not even question the whiteness of Jesus' pictures posted in every nook and cranny in their own black churches. Is it as Gunnar Myrdal wrote, "God and the angels are ordinarily white to Negroes as they are to white churchgoers, therefore, it's senseless to think otherwise."[1]

Yet, there are other important issues we must investigate. They are the ambivalent theological issues built into the practices of American Christianity. And we must investigate them to be sure that our Christian attitudes are not being formed by American attitudes towards Christianity.

We must consider the lessons taught in black history. Black history warns against becoming caught-up in the trappings of American Christianity. For American Christianity grew out of the soils of the American system of racism and religious contradictions which produced a by-product of biblical Christianity. In other words, American Christianity is a paradox, and many ideologies and biblical interpretations of black worship style and preaching grew out of the deep ambivalence found in American Christianity. In a sense, the Black Power movement of the 60's is not only an indictment against an unjust system as was the Civil Rights Movement, but also both are indictments against the practices of American Christianity.

For instance, history records that Negro slaves met the American Christ for the first time under extremely adverse conditions. This American Christ was met for the first time on board slave ships while the Negro slaves died by the thousands, chained and diseased, the stench

---

1 Gunnar Myrdal, <u>An American Dilemma</u>, (vol. II), p. 866.

unimaginable, and packed like sardines during Middle-Passage.

A Pastor friend visited a slave holding compound on the West Coast of Africa and witnessed the historical record of the rape and inhuman treatment of slaves awaiting their trip to the Americas. While on board ship, many female slaves were raped all night in the captains' cabins and then turned loose on deck during the day. In other words, the Negro slaves' initial introduction to this American Christianity was one of such gross horror that it is amazing, as history has demonstrated, that so many Negroes ever accepted Jesus.

Also, there are contradictions in the practices of American Christianity in need of serious investigation where once again black theology seeks to correct. Consider again, why in America under the standards of American Christianity, there is found little to no physical resemblance between black people and Jesus in the Bible?

Why, even after much theological research in order to publish theological and scientific findings to make more clear and understandable, more truthful, more factual the gospel events than ever before, that the reality of the blackness of Jesus still remains in America an illusive enigma?

And finally, why is it that a close study of the Christianity of the Bible reveals that whenever one has an encounter with the Christ in the Bible, their yoke of oppression is lifted and they are given new hope for the future. But under the practices of American Christianity, this does not happen! Rather, one finds oneself under the yoke of oppression, often leaving oneself with no hope for the future.

The difference is that biblical Christianity teaches and lives out its truths when it says, "Come to me all who labor and are heavy laden, and I will give you rest. Take my yoke upon you, and learn from me, for I am gentle and lowly in heart, and you will find rest for your souls. For My yoke is easy, and My burden is light," (Jesus, KJV). What we see is that the activities of Christ toward the people shows that what Christ says, Christ will do. But in America, even with its many themes of social equality and Christian charitable contributions, one still does not find that what America says, America will do. For in a land which boasts that America is the "Mother of Exiles" and "The Home of the Free..." black folk and many other poor folk are still singing, "*Sometimes I feel like a Motherless Child*," while still marching and chanting, "*We Shall Overcome.*" Hence, one can readily observe that there is a difference between American Christianity and biblical Christianity; the end result of American Christianity is life more oppressive, while the end result of biblical Christianity life is more abundant. In other words, we must look at the end result to determine if our Christian practices are American Christianity or biblical Christianity.

Yet, we must consider more specifically why it is so important that black people guard against the practices of American Christianity and focus more intently on the God of the Bible and how He moves in ways to relieve suffering from the land. We, therefore, need to seek this God of the Bible working in our history past. We must do this by employing Him in our worshipping experiences, integrating the tangible experiences of our history in our worship. *In turn, we must not allow American Christianity to form our attitudes and theological understanding about the Christianity of the Bible. For American Christianity will drastically reduce the desires of black people wanting to learn more about their heritage, while creating a superficial understanding (not fully able to grapple with) of the Christianity of the Bible.*

An example of such superficial grappling of the Bible results in the fact that many black people do not consider anything black in the Bible as being virtuous and godlike. For from their biblical standpoint of view, blackness to most black people is important only insomuch as it is to be avoided as something sinful and evil. For in the American Christian religious traditions, attention is focused on washing up and getting white; thus, holiness and purity comes in the color white, and when blacks read the Bible that is what they see. American Christianity conditions all its converts to think white.

As a result, black people find it very difficult to see other black people in the Bible.

Hence, this kind of theology militated against the spiritual, intellectual and the development of black awareness in blacks. It is especially militating against any and all forms of black literature that can be of help to us in understanding many things about our black religious heritage. For instance, when we search for religious literature in order to seek answers to our religious problems, we go to the wrong sources. We search: Cook Publishing Company, Moody Press, American Bible Society, Watchtower, etc... and after the search is over, one key issue still remains unanswered; the issue of the blackness of Jesus and that of the Bible characters. Why does the issue still remain? Simply because at this level of theological research, one cannot deal effectively with the black problem. For one looks for a solution from the same source which created the problem in the first place. (At this level of theological research, the theology of mid-American white religious norms, is the problem.) This level of theological research does not feature Jesus or any other character in the Bible as being black. This condition exists simply because there is a problem, in general, on the part of white people with any people-of-color in the world.

Bishop Henry McNeal Turner, in his address to the Georgia Senate September 3, 1868, protested over the expelling of 27 black Senate and House Leaders. They were expelled on the grounds that they were black. Bishop Turner protested, "that from this day to the day when God breathe the breath of life into Adam, no analogy for it can be found...never in the history of the world has a man been arraigned before a body clothed with legislative, judicial, and executive functions, charged with the offense of being black. Never in all the history of this world has a man been arraigned, charged with an offense committed by God Himself!"[2]

In other words, to say it plainly, in accordance with the actions of white American Christianity towards black people, God made a mistake in creating most of the world's population black for which white folk feel obligated to correct with their theology. In white American theology, there is not the faintest hint of blackness, except being associated with sin.

If we look to the events of early American history, which formed America's present day religious concepts, we will find more examples of the consequences of black people's encounters with the American Christ. During the slave era, in order to religiously justify the American institution of slavery and oppression of black people, whites first had to

2 H. Aptheker, A Documentary History Of The Negro People In The United States, (vol. 2), p. 569.

recondite the whiteness of their theology from the blackness of Jesus. Simply put, what had to be considered by whites, was the blackness of Jesus. For if they were to enslave black people, then to associate God and salvation with blackness posed a profound theological problem for whites who were actively enslaving black people.

Whites, therefore, had to create a theology that would put a huge gap between the blackness of people and God. In other words, the color black had to be disassociated from anything that was godlike and good, and reassociated with all that was sin and evil. The dilemma America was faced with, was how to involve the white church of America in such a way as to give spiritual and moral justification to slavery. The issue being, how is one to interpret Christianity and the enslavement of black people in a country which declared itself to be a Christian nation, *the hope of freedom and equality for all*. Hence, theological methods to do this needed to be worked out. Thus, the preaching of the theology of American Christianity became the solution. This brand of Christianity found the means by which the institution of slavery in America became part of the American Christian doctrines and thus slavery could be justified by the church with its understanding of the Bible.

Chinweizu, an African Historian wrote, "The slave was indoctrinated with a slave-making Christianity. He was given a version of Christianity, which emphasized that *slaves* should unfailingly obey their superiors. The slave was persuaded that his captors were better than he by heavenly dispensation... and with this belief instilled in him, his inclination to revolt or escape from slavery would... be restrained by his new religious consciousness; the slave would be afraid... of disobeying the supposed commands of heaven."[3]

Again, Leon F. Litwack wrote that an ex-slave testified, "Ole missus used tu read de good book tu us, Black'uns, on Sunday evenin's, but she mostly read dem places whar it says, 'sarvints obey your masters,' an' didn't stop tu splane it like de teachers;"[4]

Another classical example of this American brand of Christianity is found in Winthrop Jordan's book. He writes that as early as 1725, in a sermon witnessed by a white writer named George Berkely who wrote, "Christianity, and the embracing of the Gospel... continues persons just in the same state as it found them. The Freedom which Christianity gives, is a freedom from the bondage of sin and Satan... lust and passions, but as to blacks outward conditions, whatever that was before... whether bond or free, their being baptized and becoming a Christian... makes no manner of change in them."[5]

Again, the biblical doctrine used to support this is, "Slaves be obedient to your masters." Emphasis is on freeing the spirit while the body is still in bondage, and leaving unsolved the contradiction of a free spirit in a body in bondage. Hence, this brand of religion has many serious faults. For by its actions toward back people, it becomes:

a) An indictment theology against black people. For American Christianity treats black people as though they are a mistake made by God. Furthermore,

b) American Christianity does not, nor can it possess the theological and/or historical skills that are

---

3 Chinweizu, The West and the Rest of Us, p. 76.
4 L. F. Litwack, Been In The Storm So Long, p. 474.
5 W. Jordan, White Over Black, p. 191.

needed to seek the minds of black people in order to help them in their areas of spiritual needs. For it fails to see or remember anything good about blackness; rather it assigns all that is evil to blackness, for example, Black Friday, Black Death, Black Magic, Blacklist, Black Sabbath... and the list goes on.

c) Finally, American Christianity houses too many unanswered theological issues pertaining to the black condition.

For instance, under this brand of Christianity, the relationship between the black and white churches does not improve because there is a theological break between them... And what Dr. Martin Luther King said over three decades ago, is still just as true today, "That the most segregated day of the week is on Sunday, the most segregated hours are between 11 A.M.-1 P.M., and the most segregated institution in America is the Christian church."

Thus, as black people we must not fail to consider the importance of the blackness of Jesus and the Bible characters and what the teaching of black theology is saying to us. Neither must we fail to consider that this blackness is significant to us in that it is tied in with the whole biblical theme of liberating people from oppression... But to focus on how important biblical Christianity is to our heritage and how the activities of Jesus in the Bible rightly influence our religious activities and perceptions, we must consider three very important historical events in the black experience, and we must consider these historical events in light of how they parallel the activities of Jesus and the themes of the Christian gospel message of liberation.

First, we must consider a uniquely American religious phenomenon. In November of 1787, at the St. George's Church in Philadelphia, Pennsylvania, Richard Allen and Absalom Jones along with several other black churchmen, while on their knees praying, were threatened with physical confrontation by a group of white churchmen during the church worship services. And just as the white churchmen were about to physically remove the praying group, the prayer ended. The black group of churchmen and women, along with Richard Allen and Absalom Jones all walked out of the church. Richard Allen wrote in his book, "They were no more plagued with us in the church." "Here," he continued, "was the beginning and rise of the first African Church in America."[6] Hence, the problem with white Christians is that they hate to encounter or be confronted with the sins of their past against black people. Also, in American history, we do not see the total picture of white people in their dealings and in their past relationships with black people. We only see them as missionaries to black people. For mission work is a method whites often use to hide their guilt - not to improve relationships. They have thus erased from their theology their vicious attacks on black people which is the history of their initial encounter with all people-of-color in the world.

Again, we remember well on February 1, 1965, when Martin Luther King with 770 other black civil rights fighters were jailed in Selma, Alabama because they believed in the golden words of the Constitution that, "All men are created equal." Their commitment was to make that written principle become a living reality. Their

6 R. Allen, <u>Bishop Richard Allen, The Life, Experience and Gospel Labors</u>, p. 21-22 (out of print, original copy).

method was to teach and educate black people on the importance of black solidarity through economic control of their own goods. This method, which was the Civil Rights philosophy on non-violent direct confrontation, was to teach that this kind of black power is found on the ballot and not in the bullet. For to know the power we have through black unity, is to produce a system that can be profitable to the masses of black people suffering oppression and injustice.

Finally, we also remember on that same day, the Negro History Week became official. It, in its own way, also had its divine mandate. For it assumed responsibility for putting down ignorance in black people of their American religious and historical heritage. Its mandate was to raise the level of our black awareness and appreciation for our black heritage, through literature and lectures to black audiences. Through these efforts, we are made to become more keenly aware of our total heritage, so that we do not separate our religious experiences from our historical experiences in America.

For when we worship, and our worshipping is set apart from the knowledge of our history, then we discount God as being fully involved in our total experiences! Our worshipping is thus more rooted in rituals and the theatrics of emotionalism and we lessen our chances of gaining a better understanding of what the true liberation theme of Christian gospel is about.

But to say it plainly, these historical events all carried identical themes with that of the Christian gospel. They all confronted systems that survived on oppressing the weak and helpless and ignorant and in turn these historical events demanded the liberation of its people. These events became, for black people, actions identical with those of the Christian gospel. For both the actions of black people in their history and their fight for justice and those of the gospel, sought means to fight ignorance among its people and to free them from oppression.

Black people hated slavery, injustice and oppression, as did Jesus! However, they loved Jesus and the genuine closeness of the brotherhood of the gospel Jesus taught and they expressed their feelings in anger about being in bondage. The love they had for Jesus and the Christian gospel they expressed in song. For when black people sing songs about liberation from oppression, "O Freedom over me... Before I'll be a slave I'll be buried in my grave and go home to my Lord and be Free..." they not only express their absolute hatred for physical and spiritual bondage, but copied from the gospel of Jesus, their passionate desire to be free when He spoke, "The Spirit of the Lord is upon me, because he has anointed me to preach good news to the poor. He has sent me to proclaim release to the captives and recovering of sight to the blind, to set at liberty those who are oppressed," (Jesus).

Black people love Christianity and the message it brings about brotherhood. They sing about a deep desire to share with others who are oppressed their compassion and understanding of the liberating message found in Christianity. Thus they sing, "Lord I want to be a Christian in-a-my heart." For when the cares of our hearts are many, "The consolations of the Lord through others cheers (our) souls" (Psalms).

Black people truly love the Lord Jesus, and truly strive to be like Him... For together we sing, pouring out our souls before God;

"I want to be more like Jesus everyday
I want to walk just like Him
I want to talk just like Him
I want to live just like Him
Abundantly give just like Him
I want to be more like Jesus everyday."

Black people hate oppression just as does Jesus. When they come to know the Lord Jesus, they find a kinship between His sufferings and theirs. Black people use this knowledge, to ring up heaven and talk to God about holding back eternity a little bit longer. For like the life of Jesus, they have been in the storm of life a long time and they call on the Lord and tell Him about their sufferings. And because of their sufferings they need a little more time to get themselves together. Thus they pray:

"Lord, I've been in the storm so long.
You know I've been in the storm so long.
Oh Lord, give me more time to pray.
I've been in the storm so long."

"I am a motherless child.
Singing I am a motherless child.
Singing O Lord, give me more time to pray.
I've been in the storm so long.
Just look what shape I'm in.
Just look what shape I'm in.
Crying O Lord, give me more time to pray.
I've been in the storm so long."

(Nineteenth Century Negro Spiritual, author unknown)

February 22, 1981

Chapter Twelve

MUSIC IN THE CHURCH

1 Chronicles 15:1-2, 11-16, 22, 27

"David built houses for himself in the city of David; and he prepared a place for the ark of God and pitched a tent for it. Then David said,
   'No one but the Levites may carry the ark of God,
  for the Lord chose them to carry the ark of the Lord
    and to minister to him for ever' " (15:2).

"Then David summoned the priests... and said to them,
 'you are the heads of the Fathers' houses of the Levites;
   Sanctify yourselves, you and your brethren,
    so that you may bring up the ark of the Lord,
      the God of Israel,
    to the place that I have prepared for it.
   Because you did not carry it the first time,
   the Lord our God broke forth upon us,
    because we did not care for it
  in the way that is ordained' " (11,12).

Thus, the priests and the Levites sanctified themselves to bring up the ark of the Lord, the God of Israel. The Levites carried the ark of God upon their shoulders with poles as Moses had commanded according to the word of the Lord.

David also commanded the chiefs of the Levites to appoint their brethren as singers who should play loudly on musical instruments, on harps and lyres and cymbals to raise sounds of joy. Chenaniah, leader of the Levites in music, should direct the music for he understood it. In verse 27, David was clothed with a robe of fine linen along with the singers and the Levites who carried the ark. Both Chenaniah, the leader of the music and David wore a linen ephod.

In the study of music in the Bible, we learn that it came by way of centuries of development through many trials and situations. It was used for every conceivable occasion to include:

    a.) Family parties and celebrations, (prodigal son returning home)
    b.) Acclamation of heroes, (as with David)

We read in 1 Samuel 18 where the women of the village sang a song of triumph to David when David returned from slaying the Philistines. The writer wrote, "the women came out of all the towns of Israel, singing and dancing, to meet King Saul with tambourines, with songs of joy and with musical instruments" singing to one another as they made merry, "Saul has slain his thousands and David his ten thousands" (6, 7). Furthermore, music was used for:

    a) Kings being enthroned
    b) Harem music as in Ecclesiastes 2:8, "I got singers, both men and women, and many concubines, man's delight."
    c) Banquets and feasts, and a host of other occasions

On most occasions both men and women were used as singers, but as time passed and worshipping became more sophisticated, men were always the preferred singers in worship. History records that during the time of the second building of the Jewish Temple about 151 B.C., the Temple Choir consisted of not less than 12 adult singers and up to as many as 4,000 voices, all male between the ages of 30-50 years old. It was also during this period in which singing in the Temple became professional. Each singer underwent five years of musical training before they were allowed to sing.

Therefore, by the time King David ruled and thereafter, musicians and singers of the Temple Choir were all professionals and they were made singers in the choirs only by appointment and by the priest of the Temple. For we read in 1 Chronicles 15ff, King David, also King over the priests, commanded the Chief of the Levites (who were also priests) to appoint brethren to be singers with instruments of music by lifting up their voices with joy.

King David is also ascribed with the know-how of organizing a church choir. Historically, we learn that the organization of the musical service in the Temple began with King David's reign. To King David has been ascribed the creation of the Psalms and also the invention of "... instruments for music to the Lord which King David had made..." (2 Chr. 7:6).

Yet, we need to look at three types of songs mentioned in the Bible: Psalms, hymns and spiritual songs. Of these three, psalms are singled out as the standard for giving praises unto the Lord. And today, we need to use psalms as a standard of music for worship so those singers of religious songs for worship in the church, may have a spiritual reference point for music used in worship. What we learn from psalms are three things about worshipping God. First, they are different from any other songs of worship in that they tell of a special relationship to God being sung by a special people. Secondly, they differ in that only a special kind of people, specially conditioned by the Spirit of the Lord, can render back to God, these songs of praises and that only psalms are acceptable songs for giving due praises to the Lord. Finally, the Lord accepts psalms as valid praises due Him: "Praise the Lord! For it is good to sing praises to our God; for he is gracious, and a song of praise is seemly" (Ps. 147:1). Also, (Ps. 47-48:1;

150ff). Hence, psalms are songs of praise to God for which God receives in good favor. The singers are all redeemed of the Lord. Isaiah testified in his day, "...the redeemed of the Lord shall return, and come with singing unto Zion..." (51:11). And today we have a similar testimony when we sing, "Is thy heart right with God? Washed in the crimson blood. Cleansed and made holy honored in His glory. Right in the sight of God."

Thus, with this in mind, we can compare hymns and spiritual songs with songs of praises to God. In so doing, we can see how they compare with psalms in giving God the glory.

First of all, hymns are prayers. Prayers come from the hearts of people. Some are prayers like Jesus described, hypocritical. Others are effectual fervent prayers as James would say. Yet, in the sight of God, they are none other than unintelligent groans in need of the Spirit to boost them on to God. We read in Paul's letter to the Romans:

> "Likewise the Spirit helps us in our weakness;
> for we do not know how to pray as we ought,
> but the Spirit himself intercedes for us with
> sighs too deep for words. And he who searches
> the hearts of men knows what is the mind
> of the Spirit, because the Spirit intercedes for
> the saints according to the will of God"
> (8:26,27).

In other words, prayers, whether we sing or pray them, be they sincere or hypocritical, are in need of help from the Spirit before they ever make sense to God. Thus, God sends His Spirit to intercede to interpret and intercept our prayers. Hymns, therefore, are not likely tunes to praise

God. They are at best our prayers put to music. And a prayer from mankind, in any form, still needs help from the Spirit of the Lord. For John writes:

"Now we know that God hear not sinners; but if any man be a worshipper of God, and does his will, him he hears…" (9:31, NKJV).

One also needs to be in right relationship with God along with the Spirit before God hears them. For God said:

"…if my people who are called by my name
humble themselves, pray, seek my face,
and turn from their wicked ways,
then I will hear from heaven, and
will forgive their sin and heal their land"
(2Chr.7:14).

In other words, in praying to God, there are conditions to be met before God even hears the prayer. These conditions are found in the words; *Humble, Pray, Seek, and Turn.* When we meet these conditions, God acts. Singing hymns will not evoke the presence of the Lord without including these conditions.

Finally, there is the spiritual song. Included in this category are gospels. Both differ from hymns and psalms in that they address a personal condition. Spiritual songs are self-expressions and feelings born out of abject and contemptible conditions. Their merits are found in the purpose they serve. Their purpose is in maintaining the sanity of a people living in profound wretched conditions while enslaved under the whip of their slavemasters. Gospels, on the other hand, lean more towards personal testimonies. The singers' past and current personal experiences, mixed with traditional poetic expressions of God's unmerited grace, are expressed in gospel songs. Gospels are testimonies of what God is personally to the individual. Yet, spirituals differ further. They lean in the direction that God will rescue the wretched slave from his current dehumanizing situation. Thus, built into the language and meaning of many spirituals are escape codes for slaves to escape, undetected, the present horrible conditions of slavery in America. In other words, spirituals born on American soil during slavery took root in the institution of slavery. Spirituals were born because slavery existed. They are coded messages of what God will do to liberate the slave from his wretched conditions in America. God did it for the Hebrew children, "...and why not for everyone?" James Cone, a leading black theologian, said, "slavery meant working 15 – 20 hours a day and being beaten for showing fatigue. It meant being driven into a field three weeks after delivering a baby. It meant that your labor was worth more than your life, and if the market called for it, you were to be worked to death. It meant being whipped for crying over a fellow slave who had been killed while trying to escape."[1]

Spirituals were created out of a no escape environment. Thus, they carried what is called an eschatological overtone. In other words, this suffering will not last forever. James Cleveland put it succinctly, "This too shall pass." Thus, slaves would sing:

"Oh Freedom! I Love Thee!
And Before I Be A Slave, I'll Be Buried In My Grave,
And Go Home To My Lord And Be Free!"

Such songs had nothing to do with being freed from the

---

1 James Cone, The Spiritual And The Blues, p. 21.

sins of fornication, drinking, smoking, using profanity and other sins we call sins as defined by Western Christianity, because many Western Christians do these things and still go to church. Rather, it meant being freed one day, forever, from the shackles of human disgrace and the debasing institution of slavery. Singing spirituals lifted the slave above and beyond his present miserable conditions, into the everlasting peace of God in the eschaton. Not the eschaton of the pie-in-the-sky religious comfort zone we too often experience in our churches of today, but the freedom the slave sang about had a literal meaning of being delivered by the river – the Ohio Valley River that led to Canada, the Canaan land.

Therefore, "Swing Low…," meant escape plans were being made. The "…Sweet Chariot," meant any company of people who would help slaves to proceed North to freedom. "I looked over Jordan and what did I see," meant they were looking over the Ohio River to freedom into Canada. "A band of Angels coming after me," was Harriet Tubman and others who would sympathize with their plight and usher the escaping slave through the Underground Railroad into freedom. "Steal Away To Jesus," meant to sneak into the woods for a secret slave meeting, which would point them to freedom in the North. Black slaves were seemingly forever caught-up in a system that designated them as non-persons, non-humans, struggling daily to carve out of their wretched existence a meaning of somebodiness while in captivity. Thus, while living in a world that treated them so mean and cruel, they had heard of a place called Heaven where there aren't any bodies that are nobodies; but rather, a place where everybody is somebody. A place where the wicked would cease from troubling and the weary would be at ease. Thus, while living in this world of sorrow with no hope for tomorrow, the only link slaves had with human dignity is what they heard about in a "City Called Heaven." They would sing and comfort one another:

"I am a poor pilgrim of sorrow,
I'm in this world alone.
No hope in this world for tomorrow.
I'm trying to make Heaven my home.
My mother is gone on to pure glory.
My father is still walking in sin.
My sister and brother won't own me,
because I'm trying to get in.
Sometimes I am tossed and driven.
Sometimes I don't know where to roam.
I've heard of a city called Heaven.
I've started to make it my home."

This, therefore, is the slaves' eschaton. They were trying to salvage themselves from a physical and psychological corrupt, wanton, wicked and humanly disgraceful system; and spirituals were their songs of comfort and escape. These songs lifted them above and beyond the here and now. They were songs based on the literal visions of freedom. In them they found hope for tomorrow in a city called Heaven somewhere in the Promise Land.

Yet, there is another spiritual dimension to psalms. In Colossians and in Ephesians, psalms heads the list of the other two types of songs used for worship or for comfort. Paul says in Ephesians:

"...be filled with the Spirit, addressing one
another in psalms and hymns, and spiritual
songs and making melody to the Lord with all
your heart, always and for everything giving

200

thanks in the name of our Lord Jesus Christ to God the Father" (5:18-20).

Psalms, therefore, are not hymns or spirituals, but praises to God being sung by special people. David, the creator of psalms, the inventor of "instruments of praises to God;" the originator and organizer of the first church choir, the master teacher of church music, the anointed of the Lord, king and priest left on record that singers of psalms must first and foremost be sanctified. They must expressively and explicitly be set apart to do service in the House of the Lord without falter or without failure. They must be professionally trained and between the ages of 30-50. In other words, they must be at the age of maturity.

Finally, to be a singer of praises to the Lord, singers are always appointed to the choir. It is an office held only by appointment and not by vote. The Bible teaches that people come into God's program by means of; *a call, being sent, appointed, or elected.* Any other way is counterfeit. (Read Romans 8, 9, and 10.). In the Bible, send and forms of send is mentioned 957 times. Call is mentioned in all forms approximately 877 times; appointments 172 times, and elect (chosen) 30 times. Vote, or any form of the word vote, is not mentioned a single time in the Bible. Thus, church musicians are appointed to give praises to God. For when we start voting folk into God's program, the program is no longer a theocracy but a democracy. It is people ruled, not God's rule. The result is more problems arise than solutions found.

> I've had a lot of experiences with church choirs and I've discovered that one of the biggest problems with church choir members is basically the same with church members, that is one of attitudes.

With choir members attitudes are more compressed. Some bring an attitude to church. Some catch one while there. Others, bring one, catch one there, and thus leave with twice the attitude load.

Then David teaches us that singers of praises to the Lord must have a skilled leader. Their leader was Chenaniah; which means made by God. Put another way, the musical leaders have a double charge. Not only are they appointed by the priest, but they must be skilled and able to teach and to teach so as the singers will be able to understand what they are singing about. David writes in Psalms that singers should:

"Sing praises to God, sing praises,
sing praises unto our King,
sing praises. For God is the King of all the earth;
sing ye praises with understanding" (47:6-7).

Having done all that is required, then the singers are now awarded the merit of the position they hold by being robed with fine linen. The robe, therefore, is the ultimate crowning glory of the singer. The singer is now wholly in the Lord.

Now! they can sing with melody in their hearts to the Lord. Now! they can sing, knowing that God will accept their praises unto Him. Now! they can sing, the elect of the Lord, knowing that they are a special people unto the Lord. Now! they can sing with joy and understanding.

O for a thousand tongues to sing
My great redeemer's praise,
The glories of my God and king,

The triumphs of His grace.

My gracious master and my God,
Assist me to proclaim,
To spread thro' all the earth abroad
The honors of Thy Name.

May 15, 1977

Chapter
Thirteen

JOHN'S GOSPEL; A SPIRIT OF LIBERATION

Gospel of St. John

The cry for a Black Theology of Liberation by black radicals during the Civil Rights era, "challenged the black church beyond the models of love (or the practices of Western Christianity) as defined in the context of white Christianity and theology." Thus, the black church was justly faced with a theological dilemma. "It must reject Black Power as a content of Christian love and hereby join the white church's condemnation of Black Power advocates as being un-American and un-Christian; or the black church could accept Black Power as a social and political expression of the truth of the gospel," (The above quote taken from James Cone's lecture in New Brunswick, October 12, 1977; "Theology of Liberation of the Post-Civil Rights Era," (1960-1970)).

But, just as these two alternatives were before the black church to choose which side they would take as their stand on the issue of Christianity, so it is with John's gospel that he, the gospel chronicler, presents to his readers a gospel which implies in its content a choice between two options. The first is illustrated by a society of oppressed people who must choose between siding with an oppressive theology rising out of the Jewish synagogue which demands strict adherence to the Torah; and second, that of a liberating theological dimension of the Torah which was extracted by Jesus and mixed with his gospel of the Kingdom and including a message of liberation for oppressed people, (John 8:31, 32; 10:9; 12:46; 14:6; 20:31, etc.). In other words, just as the black churchman of America saw in the "models of (Christian) love (as) defined in the content of white Christian theology..." (Cone), a means whereby suffering and oppression were perpetuated among Blacks, the evangelist saw in the teaching of the Torah a model which did not liberate the community of faith from oppression; "For the law of the Spirit of life in Christ Jesus has set me free from the law of sin and death. For God has done what the law...could not do...(Jesus) condemned sin in the flesh..." (Rom. 8:2f RSV).

In other words, it is not by the Law that oppression is removed, but by the gospel of Jesus. Jesus the Liberator effects liberation of consciousness. Hence our old ways of looking at things are made obsolete. We are challenged by Jesus "...to use all our mental, emotional and physical energies to deny the oppression in which immoral society keeps many in chains."[1] For it is the "lamb of God who takes away the sin of the world!" (John 1:29). Thus, together the awakening of the consciousness and the taking away of the sin, liberates.

Therefore, John's gospel takes on a theological model of liberation which was shaped in the oppressed society of Jesus' day. For the very models of the Jewish religious system perpetuated oppression, just as the black church viewed the very models of Western Christianity as perpetuating oppression among blacks. Thus, as one would look to the literature of liberation theology of today as a tool which frees the oppressive conditions in the world, so it was that the evangelist John looked to Jesus and His gospel message of the Kingdom as that tool for liberating the oppressed of the society.

But the spirit of liberation in John is broad. It reaches into the social, religious, and political arenas of the total human experiences. John's gospel is a gospel, which takes root in a 'real life' situation. It is a community-oriented gospel of

---

1 Frederick Herzog, <u>Liberation Theology</u> (The Seabury Press, N.Y., 1972), p.46.

liberation addressing itself to any system, which tends to disfranchise or dispossess a people from humanity – the wretched in society. This kind of liberation begins by satisfying basic human needs and rights, which are given to all by God. In other words, while it is true that we must struggle to liberate 'self' in order to liberate society, we must also keep in mind that liberation of self involves liberation of the oppressive condition in society. The two are not separable. Therefore, in John's gospel, the individuals confronted are also representative of the problems faced by the larger community. Hence, the liberation message of John is consequently applied to the larger society – not exclusively restricted to self. Thus the gospel themes of John are those which embrace both liberation of the self from sin and at the same time acts to liberate oppression from society. The latter becomes contingent on the former.

Now in light of this, the gospel chronicler uses many contrasting stories which are written so that the reader may quickly identify the nature of oppression and the method Jesus used to liberate the oppressed. In these stories, two distinct elements of thought are countering each other. Good is contrasted with evil, darkness with light, and love with hate. Stress is on identifying the existing evils of the day by comparison to show where the elements of liberation are working in society. Hence, to identify the oppressive condition, John locates Jesus on the side of the victims of society, and the dialogue and actions, which Jesus took in each situation, becomes the means by which liberation is achieved.

Therefore, liberation can be expressed as a divine attribute of God working in Jesus. For where a system makes it quite impossible for a people to exercise their right to be free, liberation operates as that 'tool' which acts to set one free.

It also provides the means by which freedom is maintained; and for John, the gospel is such a tool.

For example, the retooling of one's mind and the establishing of new values in the minds of the oppressed, is a task which requires the services of a Liberator. Liberation must be invoked to reassure the oppressed that human freedom is human dignity and is also a divine decree. John set out to show that even where a religious system scales the land to make converts, but fails to make free a people and maintain their human dignity, it cannot be enjoined as a divine decree. For if the being of God is free(dom) so it is that freedom is inherent in His decree and in His design of creation. Therefore, all creation, and rightly so, naturally acts against all forms of human oppression. For this reason, any system rising to cancel this freedom, also at the same time, rises against God.

Yet, another point should be considered in looking for the spirit of liberation in John's gospel. One should consider that liberation is not the same as taking liberties. John is not speaking of taking liberties. Liberation for John means liberation in totality. This means the liberation of the whole society of oppressed peoples. It also means the liberation of the whole self from the traditional grounds of maintaining the status quo by being a part of a system, which victimize some and gives its graces to others (as in the Nicodemus story which will be discussed below). Hence, it means to be completely liberated from the sins of "private selfhood."[2]

---

2   According to Herzog, as a Western man we are still "utterly private selves," and "Christology in terms of the fourth gospel is a radical attack upon our isolation." We must therefore learn to incorporate self within the total society, in which we live, and learn the part of being liberated "from the make-believe world of the private self." Furthermore, sin has many faces. It is not just found in the shadows of the "private selfhood," but it is also a displaced relationship with God. It negates freedom and gives vent to oppression. Sin is the "yielding to oppression," (pgs.81-91). However, in light of its many faces and encroaching areas of our lives, it "is not an eternal reality...it is man's pseudocreation. Jesus' liberation curbs sin's power. He embodies a new direction of our destiny..."(p.120).

In John's gospel, "Jesus is concerned about a different self, corporate selfhood, which man controls as little as the wind...the private I no longer prevails" (Herzog, p.62). For the taking of liberties does not seek this route. In a world besieged with social, political and religious anxieties, "...men if not peoples prefer liberties to liberty..."[3] in order to relieve social anxieties. In other words, liberties are often preferred over liberty. For it tends to give one extra civil status, without making them accountable to the total society. It will further enable them to cope with their anxieties to the exclusion of others. Thus to take liberties, "leaves unconsidered the issues of national (total) liberation..." (Chinweizu, p.98) from oppression. But when liberated, the kind which the gospel is speaking of, it becomes necessary for one to construct a new society. It means to be *born anew.* It is a new reality which will compel one "to view himself other than he is" (Herzog, p.63). For example; John 3 is the story of Nicodemus, "a leader of the Jews who came to Jesus by night." According to Herzog, if the Nicodemus story could be read so that anyone reading the Nicodemus story could feel the impact of what it means to be *born anew,* verses 3, 4, and 7 would read; vs. 3; "Jesus answered, believe me, no man can see the kingdom of God unless he becomes white/black." vs 4; "Nicodemus wondered, how can a man become white/black when he is white/black?" "Do not be surprised that I told you, you must become black;" whereby black is substituted for *"born anew;"* then one can better come to understand through cultural shock what it means to have to wrestle with a problem like Nicodemus in trying to reconcile in his mind, how he can still remain part of the system which oppresses and yet not be one of the oppressors. Hence, the radicality of Jesus' message to Nicodemus, "you must be *born anew,"* is an expression

---

3   Chinweizu, The West And The Rest Of Us, (Vintage Books, N.Y. 1975, p.97).

that liberation should become so compelling that it will cause "one to view himself other than he is" (Herzog, p.63). To Nicodemus, to be *"born anew"* is to give up completely the glamour of being the oppressor. Thus the liberating message of Jesus to Nicodemus, is that Nicodemus must become completely liberated from the very system he has come to love and internalize. In other words, Nicodemus cannot be of a system, which oppresses any more than Jesus was of the system, which oppressed people. In other words, the black church cannot be of a system, which oppresses.

Furthermore, Jesus and the Nicodemus story also typify the struggles of a people fighting within themselves to become free from the disease of internalizing too deeply the values and norms of the society which is oppressing them. They have a strong desire to be freed from its oppressive system, but yet do not have the tools to free themselves. For the system which oppresses them, did not supply them with the means to be free. Therefore, any attempt on their part to improve their condition, could only act to worsen their condition; such a people is not equipped to free themselves.

Thus, this kind of spiritual ambiguity is manifested in the dialogue between Jesus and Nicodemus. For the system which drove Nicodemus to search for Jesus under the "concealment of night"[4] is also the same system which

---

4   According to Herzog, "Man's self-concealment expresses itself in the gloom of the mind, in inner darkness. Sin is the gloom of self-concealment from God and fellow man in the privacy of the private self" (p.121). The encroachment upon one under the concealment of night is demonstrative of one not wanting "to associate with the light, open life" (p.122). One of man's greatest sins according to Herzog, is to be concealed in his own private self, as demonstrated in the Nicodemus story. Thus liberation is achieved when man is able to break out of this bag of privatism and self-concealment from humankind. Jesus invites people to break loose from this "sin-bag,' for "man's self inflicted fate is that he dies in his sin, his self-concealment in privatism" (p.123). He denies corporate life, he prefers darkness to light. His life is not future oriented in that it would embody the whole of humankind, but rather turn inward to self. To Herzog, "This is dying to sin" (p.123).

gave him position and status, and recognition as "a teacher." It was a system, which treated him well as long as he would continue to oppress the weak. This, Nicodemus could not reconcile in his mind, thus he sought escape; Jesus said, "Do not marvel that I said to you 'you must be [liberated from any system which oppresses the weak and the victims of society, and this you must do by being] *born anew.*' " To this Nicodemus sought escape: "How can this be?" Thus the liberation message to Nicodemus was for him to disrobe completely of the ambiguities in his life and become robed again in a whole new system of things – to be "*born anew.*"

The message of John then, is that of becoming something entirely new. There is a transformation, a psychic metamorphosis, a new beginning. The overriding motif of the gospel suggests that liberation is the start of a new beginning or a new application to Christianity. An example of this is that of Jesus and the Samaritan woman. Jesus opens up to her the possibilities of a new beginning rather than making an attempt to reconcile the broken pieces of her past life. He does this by unfolding before her the history of her life: "Come see a man who told me all that I ever did." The offer Jesus makes her is one of a complete new self: "...whoever drinks of the water that I shall give...will never thirst..." Thus John is showing how liberation even works for the least in society giving new respect and dignity even to those considered "non-persons" in an oppressive society. For according to Herzog, "Segregation between Jews and Samaritans had lasted more than four-hundred years by the time Jesus appeared...What is more, the woman was not very respectable. Finally she was a woman...(and) strict rabbis did not speak to women in public, some not even to their own wives" (p.73). Yet again, Jesus acted contrary to social norms in order that the "walls between persons would come tumbling down." Thus, the new beginning Jesus offers the woman is in the word "*whoever.*" In other words, never before has the gulf between Jews and Samaritans, Jews and women been bridged. The single event between Jesus and the Samaritan woman started a new relationship in the total human family. Here, human liberation is acting against color discrimination, group segregation, oppression of women, and for the "not very respectable ones" in a society.

Another example is the raising of Lazarus as a liberation act of a new beginning. This story demonstrates a complete separation from the impossible entanglement of the past. In this episode, John shows that liberation from even the most hopeless situation is not an impossibility. This story typifies a kind of people so downtrodden in society that it results in 'death.' Hence the evangelist shows that there is an oppression in which no political system, however just, can legislate liberty. Yet John demonstrates that even under circumstances such as these, one can still be liberated; but only by divine intervention. Lazarus,[5] whom Jesus loves, is

---

5 It may be difficult to ascertain with any degree of certainty that Lazarus himself was poor and oppressed in his society. But however, Chapter 11:1 does tell us four things about him which might give the reader some insight into his social climate and living condition. First; Lazarus was not just any man but he was a "certain man" who secondly; "was ill." Thirdly; the name Lazarus means "God helps" John Marsh, Saint John, p.420, and fourthly; Lazarus was from a village of Bethany. Thus to start with the fourth point, Bethany is a "Semitic derivation" meaning "...house of the poor, afflicted..." It is also "the setting for the story about Simon the leper..." (I.D.B., Vol. I, p.387f). Next, the name Lazarus may suggest symbolically that because of his wretched condition in Bethany (house of the poor), Lazarus was in desperate need of 'God's help.' Certainly this would coincide with point two in that he "was ill." Finally, the report could very well single out Lazarus, a "certain man" as being symbolic of the social ills heaved upon him. Therefore only a "certain man" could qualify in such desperation as to receive special help from God. Furthermore, according to Herzog, the resurrection of Lazarus is symbolic of "unoppressed manhood." *Jesus* "sets man free from the powers that keep him in ultimate bondage" (Herzog, p.158). Could it be that Lazarus is a symbol of total human depravity, which has gone beyond healing – thus resurrection? Maybe one should even consider what Lazarus' life was like in Bethany before Jesus knew him.

representative of the poor, the oppressed, hungry, captives and blind lost victims of society beyond human hope. Jesus thus demonstrates his power as Liberator in the Lazarus story as one who is able even to liberate the most wretched in society, giving them new beginning. One can be resurrected unto a new life no matter how hopeless the situation may be. Liberation therefore, in a sense, is resurrection.[6] It is the fulfilling of the over-powering desire to be free. In John's gospel, this desire even reaches beyond human comprehension. The liberating power of Jesus can liberate one from the most hopeless conditions.

In John, there were many Nicodemuses, Samaritan women, and Lazaruses. Many were in need and in search of a radical change in their lives like Nicodemus. Many needed a new beginning like the Samaritan woman, and there were even those so downtrodden that a resurrection unto new life like Lazarus' suited their case. But they all suffered a system which needed a "bringing into being of that which is not..."[7] Many needed a "justice that remains discontented unless it includes all" and this new state of being is "at once so radical and so impossible a demand as rightly to be called a resurrection of the dead..."[8]

Thus, these archetype characters that John portrays in his gospel are drawn from the massive system of corruption and oppression flooding the times of Jesus. How much easier the gospel would have been, had Jesus viewed the

---

6 Liberation according to Herzog, is truly human. To be human is to be liberated. For it is in the concealment of the private self that man is in bondage. "What makes man truly human is freedom." Liberation is Jesus inviting men to see their end, in the darkness of the private self. The hope of liberation is their ability to realize their present fate, if they continue in sin, and thereby see the hope of liberation from their sin in Jesus.

7 Peter Selby, Look For The Living, (Fortress Press, Phil., 1976), Chapter 6.

8 Ibid., p.171.

whole of the system as worthy of total destruction and acted accordingly. What if John wrote his gospel account from the perspective of a new beginning created by Jesus in order to rid the world of all oppression?

But according to John, the need to destroy completely and create anew, in order to bring about a new order was not in the ministry of Jesus. Rather, His ministry was to completely liberate and start a new life in the lives of those corrupted by oppression. So it is that the teachings of our black churches must be the same!

Hence, John's gospel leads us to note that liberation is the choice between evil and good, light and darkness, the old system and the new Kingdom. The black church of today is, therefore, faced with the challenge of a similar choice. It must move beyond the models of love and Christianity as defined and practiced by the white church in America; or "accept Black Power as a social and political expression of the truth of the gospel" (Cone), and chose to follow the models of love and Christianity as defined in the gospel of Jesus. Thus, it was with the oppressed in Jesus' day that they had also to choose between a religious system which kept them oppressed and that of the liberating message of Jesus' gospel as recorded by John. For we are free only in so much as we share in the words of Jesus and open up to the message of liberation found in the gospel of St. John. For John presents Jesus as the Liberator with the message of liberation. It is the opening up to Jesus and not the turning to another system, which is the liberation that set men free:

"The man from whom the demons had gone begged that he might be with him; but he sent him away, saying, 'Return to your home, and declare how much God has done for you.' And he went away, proclaiming throughout the whole city how much **JESUS HAD DONE** for him" (Luke 8:38,39).

December 13, 1977

Chapter
Fourteen

HAVE YOU LOOKED AT
YOUR SPIRITUAL LIFE LATELY?

Ezekiel 37:1-14

"The hand of the Lord was upon me, and He brought me out by the Spirit of the Lord, and set me down in the midst of the valley; it was full of bones" (Ezekiel 37:1).

The Word of God teaches us that man is confronted constantly with death both physically and spiritually. In the book of Ezekiel, the prophet observed how Israel died both deaths and had become "dry bones, clean cut off" from God.

However, the mysticism of Ezekiel's vision is not about death, but about the difference between physical life and spiritual life in God. Israel is physically alive, but, without the spirit of God. Ezekiel observes this when the God of Israel takes him to the valley of dry bones to show him "these bones" in which God "will cause breath to enter" and they "shall live."

> "Thus says the Lord God to these bones:
> Behold, I will cause breath to enter you,
> And you shall live" (5).

God being mindful of the flesh and spirit of man, shows Ezekiel how He first deals with the physical life form of man then puts His Spirit within. Step by step He forms man, "I will lay sinews upon you, and will cause flesh to come upon you, and cover you with skin, and put breath in you, and you shall live" (6).

Israel, "You shall live" and that's all. Alive, but without

purpose, without meaning, without hope. For your sins have left you spiritually dead, divided asunder, scattered, with no hope. Without His Spirit, Israel is "dry bones" covered with sinews, flesh, and skin. Yet, God breathed "upon these slain, that they may live."

Israel is "upon their feet, an exceedingly great host." There they stand, a testimony to their own contemptible and wretched ways; yet empty, destitute, as castaways, and doomed. They say, "our bones are dried up, and our hope is lost; we are clean cut off" for when the Spirit of God is removed from a person though they be alive – they are actually dead. Such is the way of God. Time and again the prophets of old record that the absence of the Spirit of God is spiritual death. Isaiah wrote, "that our iniquities separate us from God" and that He hides His face from us if we sin and "will not hear." Paul's advice to Timothy concerning widows who prefer a life of pleasure to "supplications and prayers" is, "she that lives in pleasure is dead while she lives." And our Lord put it very candidly when He said, "Follow me and let the dead bury the dead."

So it was in the days of Ezekiel, when he saw "the whole house of Israel" as "bones dried up" because they refused to obey God. The Spirit of God was not with them. They wanted to have their own way. But their consequences were like that of a ship tossed about in a raging sea. It will eventually be smashed against the rocks. So it was with Israel. After being tossed about in the raging sea of life, she was smashed on the valley floor, as smoldering "dry bones." Now! There they stand. "An exceedingly great host." *Alive, but for what? Ready to go somewhere, but where? Clean cut off! No purpose! No direction! No hope! Alive, yet dead!*

But, "The hand of the Lord was upon me" for yet another reason. Ezekiel is shown the peculiar way in which God will unite the divided kingdom of Israel. A house divided against itself cannot stand – for the Spirit of the Lord unites. *In God there is no division*! God told Ezekiel to "prophesy" so that the Spirit of the Lord could work and unite Israel. He did. And the noisy rattling of bones was heard as they came together. The Spirit of the Lord was working to bring Israel together - restored unto the Lord!

It was at this point that this awe-inspired prophet saw New Hope for Israel. As God worked, Ezekiel watched. For in the Lord life is renewed. There is unity, togetherness and brotherhood. The Spirit revives, renews, and restores us unto God thus, not for long will Israel be in exile. Not long will they be estranged from God. Not long will they be as scattered sheep, bones dried up, hope lost, "clean cut off." By the mercies of God, Ezekiel was to prophesy so that the "whole house of Israel" will live together and be restored unto God. For "behold" as "bones came together, bone to its bone" so shall Israel come together, united under one Kingdom, restored unto God.

But that's not all. Again the "hand of the Lord was upon me" to show Ezekiel another mystery. It's the mystery of a spirit-filled life, filled with the glory of God. God was showing Ezekiel that when He put His Spirit in Israel, Israel would have life and live more abundantly - the kind of life that causes us to move, live and have our being in God. It is a God-conscious life. A life that causes us to love and care about our neighbors. It knits our hearts into a fine network of mutuality. We are, therefore, able to feel what our neighbors feel. Suffer with them. Rejoice with them. It is the type of life that creates in our thinking a concept of togetherness, and an awareness of others. A life whereby we work together, build together, live together, worship together, because it is in the Spirit of God that we exist together - it is a Spirit-filled life that gives us the awareness that our lives are mutually tied in with the destiny of our fellowman, and that the anguish of one, diminishes the joy of all.

It is the Spirit of God that does all these things. It requires that our lives become more meaningful and connected. What was to be life in the flesh is now transformed into a life filled with the abundance of His Spirit. It is that Spirit within that makes all the difference in the world.

The story is told of a young seminarian graduate recently installed as pastor in a local church. After eloquently quoting the 23rd Psalm in his best seminary trained manner to his congregation one Sunday, he felt rather let-down because he did not get the response he had anticipated. A few Sundays later, a much older member of his church was called upon to pray. He selected the same Psalm. When he finished saying the Psalm in his own ungrammatical and inarticulate style, many tearful sobs and amen rose from the floor. Sometime later it was revealed to the young pastor that there is something in the way in which something is said that will trigger an active response. Later the pastor came to realize, that although he quoted the 23rd Psalm eloquently, coloring every word with its proper tint according to his academic training, he had only succeeded in gaining the respect of a good story teller. However, the old gentleman had spoken the 23rd Psalm as though he had lived it. He added that necessary dimension to the Psalm that made it come alive in the hearts of many. He did this by putting his experience in the Psalm. He became the one who "walked through the shadow of death," and many of his parishioners walked with him.

When God puts His Spirit in us, our lives are made anew. We are alive with meaning and purpose. We become "new creatures." So it was the same with Israel. The Spirit of God gave them a great awakening. A spiritual awakening in that God put His Spirit within them, and gave them new hope so that they "shall live" and grow stronger in their "own land." With this Spirit they shall "know that I, the Lord, have spoken," and "open your graves and raise you ... put my Spirit within... (brought) you home into the land of Israel ... that they may live." How wonderful it is to know that the Spirit of God is *life*.

However, there is a final lesson to be learned from Ezekiel, the lesson of togetherness. "The hand of the Lord was upon me" that Ezekiel might behold the works of the Spirit. Judah and Ephraim are turned away from each other. They are politically divided and because of their division, God is a God "clean cut off" from them. Only through united Israel, will God work His eternal purpose. God is a God of unity, not conflict.

So it is today. Just as God could not work with part of Israel, neither can He work with part of our lives. Just as Israel must be united and become one kingdom, so our lives must be surrendered wholly to His will, "not in part but the whole." Just as God is calling Israel back unto Himself "that they may live" and serve Him, so it is today that the same call goes forth to us, that we might repent and have eternal life in Christ. A people who have wandered far from God, lost in a world of political difference, economical exploitation, poverty, and fear, is none the better than the "valley of dry bones" Ezekiel saw. As it was in the days of Ezekiel that God, in His mercies, saw fit to knit together the hearts of Israel to worship and serve Him, so it is today. He sees fit to work through the hearts of Christian men and women, to knit together the mammoth gap of spiritual cleavage between our black and white churches, so that Christians may come to grip with the problem of racism and religious differences in the House of God.

The question still remains. Are our lives wholly in Spiritual unity with Christ, or are we today, the church in America, as in the days of Ezekiel, a "valley of dry bones"? If the hand of the Lord is upon us, and He brings us out into our communities by His Spirit and sets us down in the midst of them, will we find them full of "dry bones"?

January 7, 1976

Chapter
Fifteen

NOTES ON ABRAHAM

Genesis 15

"The Old Testament does not always make sense, and what sense it does make offends modern ears. For these and other reasons, the O.T., which is three-fourths of the Bible, often goes unread." "Polls show that 80% of Americans claim to believe in the Ten Commandments, but very few can name as many as four of them. Half of all adult Americans cannot identify the Bible's first book as Genesis" and fewer yet do not realize that the writing of Job pre-dates the writing of Genesis. In a recent poll, "14%" of the 80% of Americans, who claimed to believe in the Ten Commandments but could not name four of them, "identify Joan of Arc as Noah's wife."[1]

What we learn from the Bible, which too often is contrary to our cultural norms of Bible learning, is that for leading biblical persons like Abraham, Joseph, Moses and David, "...God moves in ways we would not predict or even desire."[2]

Too often, people do not discriminate between conscious blind obedience to God and the thoughtless and indiscriminate obedience to anything else which per-chance in their habits of indiscriminate obedience, they may just so happen to obey God.

The conscious blind obedience is a deliberate and conscious effort of obedience initiated on the part of the individual to obey God, being fully aware of the

---

1 Philip Yancy, <u>The Bible Jesus Read, p. 18.</u>
2 Ibid., p. 32.

consequences involved and they are willing to suffer should they disobey.

The thoughtless indiscriminate obedience is the indiscriminate autonomic behavioral response of the individual who will behave in certain ways all the time under given situations, be it good or bad. Individuals, under these circumstances, make no deliberate conscious effort to obey God neither do they prepare ahead for any consequences occurring as a result of their behavior. Their behavioral responses are by force of habit, or autonomic behavioral responses. What must be considered, for God to enter into a covenant with anyone at this level of indiscriminate behavior, becomes a threat to any covenant made between God and humanity. God, as we shall see, guards against this indiscriminate act of behavior.

Below are my responses to the above discussion pertaining to Abraham's autonomic behavior.

Abraham's thoughtlessness of God's Covenant

Abraham, as with anyone, was a victim of autonomic behavioral response - a form of indiscriminate behavior. His reaction to the Abraham/Isaac sacrifice event was rooted in his cultural behavior as seen by his decision to go to Egypt (Gen. 12:10-19). He came from a culture that not only practiced wife stealing but also a culture that practiced infanticide. This indiscriminate behavior of practicing infanticide was rooted in his culture. Abraham did what he did all along, that was to practice his indiscriminate behavior. The choice he made to sacrifice his son was by his autonomic behavioral response. In other words, Abraham had no thought of himself being righteous, neither was he sure of what he was about to do in terms of his willingness to give away so quickly the *promise*. But God being God was fully aware of Abraham's behavior, therefore, we find in (15:7-21) a most strange covenant which precedes the Abraham/Isaac event and further demonstrates how God guards against intrusting His Covenant in the hands of humanity. The intervention of God's grace prevented Abraham from sacrificing his son.

What we know about ancient cultures' covenant making is: *"Normally both parties making the covenant would walk together between the pieces of the animals rendering the terms mandatory on both parties. If one failed to keep his terms, it would free the other from keeping his. In this way, the covenant was conditional. In this case, however, it was not God and Abraham who walked between the pieces of the animals, but God alone, binding only Himself to the terms of the Covenant. This rendered the Covenant unconditional. Its fulfillment is based purely on God's grace regardless of how often Abraham or his seed may fail."*[3]

What must be considered at this point is that any fulfillment of an eternal covenant initiated by God can only be valid and unconditional *"if its fulfillment were divorced from human responsibility"*[4] and the covenant terms must depend upon God alone, to be unconditional.

Genesis 22:5

In (22:5) many ancient and modern apologist have surmised that Abraham's response to his "young men" accompanying him was made under duress. For instance,

---

3 Arnold G. Fruchtenbaum, <u>Israelology</u>, p. 345.
4 Ibid., p. 345.

they surmised:

- He was lying to the servants to buy time...maybe to figure out another approach to explain his actions.
- He was suffering from delusion and no longer speaking rationally...because the trauma was too great for him to deal with.
- He believed that he and the boy would return.[5]

What must be realized from the above is God's attribute to His own righteousness being imputed to the activity of Abraham. Said another way, "Abraham was not justified by works." [As in the above, his interest was trying to relieve himself of the pressure he was under.] "God made a promise to Abraham, and Abraham trusted God to fulfill it. Because of Abraham's faith, God credited Abraham with righteousness. In gaining this righteousness from God, Abraham did not obey some law or perform some ritual like circumcision, he simply believed God."[6] This is an act of God's saving grace working in Abraham.

> God's grace active in the Abraham/Isaac
> event has precedence over the strength
> of Abraham's faith and obedience

Thus, what we see in this event of the sacrifice of Isaac is the intervention of God's grace in the indiscriminate autonomic behavior patterns of Abraham, which was in constant operation in his belief system. He is already culturally conditioned to infanticide. Hence, to practice infanticide for the Lord would be no different from practicing infanticide for his own culture.

In other words, as we are today all under the grace of God, no matter what we do, so it was with Abraham. What

---

5 Nelson's New Illustrated Bible Commentary, p. 43.
6 Ibid., p. 1430.

must be considered is this: At what level of spirituality was Abraham's knowledge of God, at this point in his life, after having already attempting several times in the past to make void the *promise* of God?

What is being demonstrated by the Genesis writer is that God is being true to His promise to Abraham and that it is God who must take the action to preserve His promise in us (Genesis 15:17,18).

What is further being recorded in this scenario is God's grace being played out in the bad behavior of Abraham. *We must be careful not to override God's grace with Abraham's bad behavior patterns. To say it another way, God's grace is superior to our faith in and our obedience to Him.* God's grace working in our bad behaviors is one thing while "let this mind be in you which is in Christ Jesus," is another. Abraham had not reached that level of spiritual development.

The position of the New Testament (N. T.)

The N. T. wants its readers to assume that of the latter, "let this mind be in you..." because Jesus is now come and gone to bring in that new behavior, i.e., the Kingdom of God. Hence, what the N. T. is pointing to in attributing faith to Abraham in the book of Hebrews, is the position we all are to assume since the coming of Jesus. The God/Abraham event is used as a model for the faith of the N. T. Church. (See Heb. 11:17-19).

The Abraham/Isaac story is being used as an example for the foundation of the Christian church (see Eph.2:8-10). Notice the quote "this is not your own doing..." To say it another way, Abraham did not have faith, obedience, righteousness in and of his "own doing."

Hence, the point to be made is not that Abraham was so great, but rather God's grace was greater in Abraham causing Abraham to be great in God's grace, "My grace is sufficient for you, for My power is made perfect in [your] weakness" (2 Cor. 12:9).

The N. T. is focusing on the spirit of faith in the church, which comes out in the events of God's interaction and interventions with the personalities of the O. T., to include Abraham. Hence, Paul concluded, "All who believe, as did Abraham, become heirs to the fulfillment of the promises in Christ"[7] (also read Gal. 3:28,29). To Paul, there is no other way to salvation except that which was inaugurated in Abraham by the grace of God.

Some things to consider about Abraham

We realize, without a doubt that Abraham stands out as a landmark in the spiritual history of the world. His original name, Abram means the same as Abraham "father of heights" or "father of a multitude." Although he was chosen of God, Abraham "was not much to make him worthy of such distinction." "His choice was one of God's grace."[8]
- He was a Gentile.
- He uttered no prophecy, wrote no books, sang no songs, gave no laws.
- He was subject to many failures, yet,
- In the long list of Bible saints, he alone is spoken of as, "father of the faithful...and the friend

---

7 The New World Dictionary Concordance to the New American Bible, p 8.
8 Herbert Lockyer, All The Men of The Bible, p. 28.

of God"[9] (Is. 41:8). All this was by means of God's grace.

Symbolism

- Isaac made to carry his own sacrificial wood/Jesus carrying his own cross
- Isaac, the only son of Abraham (22:2-4)/Jesus the only son of God
- Isaac's dialogue with his father Abraham (22:7,8)/Jesus' dialogue with His father on Calvary
- Isaac's supreme confidence in his father and also his willing consent to become the victim/Jesus' supreme confidence in His father who gave Himself for our sins

July 21, 1999

---

9 Ibid.

Bibliography

Allen, Diogenes. *Christian Belief in a Postmodern World.* Louisville:Westminster/John Knox Press, 1989.

Allen, Richard. *The Life Experience and Gospel Labors of The Rt. Rev. Richard Allen.* (1888) (Out of Print) (see; George, Carol V. R. *Segregated Sabbaths.* New York: Oxford University Press, Inc., 1973).

Anderson, Bernhard W. *Out of the Depths.* 2nd ed. Philadelphia: Westminster, 1977.

Aptheker, Herbert, ed. *A Documentary History of The Negro People in The United States.* 2 vols. Secaucus, N.J.: The Citadel Press, 1972.

Chinweizu. *The West and the Rest of Us.* New York: Vintage Books, 1975.

Cone, James H. *The Spiritual and the Blues.* New York: The Seabury Press, 1972.

Fruchtenbaum, Arnold G. *Israelology, The Missing Link in Systematic Theology*, Tustin, Calif: Ministries Press, 1992.

Harding, Vincent. *There is a River.* New York: Vintage Books, 1981.

Heffner, Richard D. *A Documentary History of The United States.* New York: The New American Library, 1952.

Herzog, Frederick. *Liberation Theology.* New York: The Seabury Press, 1972.

Jordan, Winthrop D. *White Over Black.* Baltimore: Penguin Books, Inc. 1971.

Kittel, Gerhard, ed. *Theological Dictionary of the New Testament.* Vol. IV. Grand Rapids: William B. Eerdman's Publishing Company, 1967. (Reprint 1977).

Litwack, Leon F. *Been in the Storm.* New York: Random House, 1979.

Lockyer, Herbert. *All the Men of the Bible.* Grand Rapids, Michigan: Zondervan Publishing House, 1958.

Myrdal, Gunnar, ed. *An American Dilemma.* 2 vols. New York: Pantheon Books, 1972.

The New World **Dictionary Concordance** *to the New American Bible*, Library of Congress Catalog Card Number 72-77415, International Standard Book Number 0-529-04540-0, manufactured in the United States of America: C. D. Stampley Enterprises, Inc., 1970.

Selby, Peter. *Look for the Living* Philadelphia: Fortress Press, 1976.

Snowden, Frank M. Jr. *Blacks in Antiquity: Ethiopians in The Greco-Roman Experience.* Cambridge, Massachusetts: Harvard University Press, 1970.

Stagg, Frank. *New Testament Theology.* Nashville: Broadman Press, 1962.

Thiessen, Henry C. *Lectures in Systematic Theology.* Grand Rapids: William B. Eerdman's Publishing Company, 1979. (Reprint 1997).

Vischer, Lukas. *Tithing in the Early Church.* Philadelphia: Fortress Press, 1966.

Yancy, Philip. *The Bible Jesus Read.* Grand Rapids, Michigan: Zondervan Publishing House, 1999.

Commentaries
Brown, R. E., Kitzmyer, J. A., Murphy, R. E., *The Jerome Biblical Commentary.* 2 vols. Carm, D. ed. (Englewood Cliffs, New Jersey: Prentice-Hall, Inc., 1968).

Nelson's New Illustrated Bible Commentary. Rademacher, Earl D., Allen, Ronald B., House, H. Wayne, eds. (Nashville, Tennessee: Thomas Nelson Publishers, 1999).

Stern, David H., *Jewish New Testament Commentary.* (Clarksville: Jewish New Testament Publications, Inc., 1999).

Chapter Scriptual Index

Chapter 1. The Blackness Of The Bible
Genesis 29:25; 31:41
Exodus 4:6; 16:31
Numbers 12:10
2Kings 5:1ff
Song Of Solomon 1:5; 2:1; 5:10
Esther 1:6; 8:15;
Matthew 3:27; 5:36; 23:27
Mark 9:3
Acts 13:1; 17:16,22,23; 18:23b; 21:37,38; 23:3
Revelation 6:8

Chapter 2, Manhood:
Genesis 1:27; 2:5-8,18,20,21,22; 3:1-5,16-20; 29:31,32
Exodus 20:4; 21:10
Isaiah 1:5b; 3:25-41
Jeremiah 17:9a
Ezekiel 24:15-18
Psalm 139:ff
Proverbs 9:13; 21:9; 31:10ff
Romans 3:ff; 6:23a; 13:8-10
Ephesians 5:21ff
Titus 2:4,5
1John 4:7-12
1Corinthians 7:14
2Corinthians 6:14

Chapter 3, It's Time To Wake-Up:
Psalm 46:1
Jeremiah 32:27
Luke 4:18
Romans 13:11

Chapter 4. Insights Into Tithes And Tithing:
Genesis 3:4,5,17; 14:17-20; 28:18-22
Exodus 33:19ff
Leviticus 27:1-3,26-30
Numbers 12:6-8; 14:13,14; 18:21-24; 30:1,2
Deuteronomy 14:28,29; 23:21-23
1Samuel 8:15,17
1Chronicles 29:6-14
2Chronicles 7:14; 29:10-16,29ff
Psalm 50:1-15
Isaiah 1:1-10ff; 2:3; 30:9; 43:23
Jeremiah 18:18; 23:23-32; 28:ff
Ezekiel 18:32
Amos 4:4,5
Micah 6:8
Malachi 1:1,2,6,11-14; 2:1,2,7,8,10-14,17-3:4ff; 3:1-5,6-15
Matthew 5:7; 6:24,33; 21:12,13; 17:24-27; 19:16-24; 22:36-40; 23:23,24;
Mark 7:1-13
John 1:17,19ff; 3:16; 10:10; 14:26
Luke 4:18-21; 11:42; 16:13; 18:10ff
Acts 2:43-47; 4:32-37; 5:1-11; 8:18-22ff; 20:35
Romans 12:6-10
2Corinthians 9:7
Galatians 3:10-26; 4:4,5
Hebrews 6:1; 7:8-10

Chapter 5. Spiritual Blindness:
1Corinthians 13:ff
1Timothy 5:24

Chapter 6. Let's Get Married!:
Genesis 2:16-18; 3:ff

Chapter 13. John's Gospel: A Spirit Of Liberation:
John 1:29; 8:31,32; 10:9; 12:46; 14:6; 20:31
Romans 8:2ff

Chapter 14. Have You Looked At Your Spiritual Life Lately?
Ezekiel 37:1,5,6

Chapter 15. Notes On Abraham:
Genesis 12:10-19; 15:7-21; 22:2-8
Isaiah 41:8
2Corinthians 12:9
Galatians 3:28,29
Hebrews 11:17-19
Ephesians 2:8-10

To Order Book(s)

Thee of Come Things All... (ISBN 0-9703823-5-9)

Name _____

Address _____ Apt.# _____

City/State/Zip _____

Number of books _____

Send check or money order payable to "**LightHouse Press**" for $14.00 per book. Plus **$3.95** shipping and handling to:

LightHouse Press
P.O. Box 281375
Nashville, TN 37228

Please allow 2-3 weeks for delivery.

To Order Book(s)

Thee of Come Things All... (ISBN 0-9703823-5-9)

Name _____

Address _____ Apt.# _____

City/State/Zip _____

Number of books _____

Send check or money order payable to "**LightHouse Press**" for $14.00 per book. Plus **$3.95** shipping and handling to:

LightHouse Press
P.O. Box 281375
Nashville, TN 37228

Please allow 2-3 weeks for delivery.

To Order Book(s)

Thee of Come Things All... (ISBN 0-9703823-5-9)

Name _____

Address _____ Apt.# _____

City/State/Zip _____

Number of books _____

Send check or money order payable to "**LightHouse Press**" for $14.00 per book. Plus **$3.95** shipping and handling to:

LightHouse Press
P.O. Box 281375
Nashville, TN 37228

Please allow 2-3 weeks for delivery.

To Order Book(s)

Thee of Come Things All... (ISBN 0-9703823-5-9)

Name _____

Address _____ Apt.# _____

City/State/Zip _____

Number of books _____

Send check or money order payable to "**LightHouse Press**" for $██ per book. Plus **$3.95** shipping and handling to:

LightHouse Press
P.O. Box 281375
Nashville, TN 37228

Please allow 2-3 weeks for delivery.

To Order Book(s)

Thee of Come Things All... (ISBN 0-9703823-5-9)

Name _____

Address _____ Apt.# _____

City/State/Zip _____

Number of books _____

Send check or money order payable to "**LightHouse Press**" for $██ per book. Plus **$3.95** shipping and handling to:

LightHouse Press
P.O. Box 281375
Nashville, TN 37228

Please allow 2-3 weeks for delivery.

To Order Book(s)

Thee of Come Things All... (ISBN 0-9703823-5-9)

Name _____

Address _____ Apt.# _____

City/State/Zip _____

Number of books _____

Send check or money order payable to "**LightHouse Press**" for $██ per book. Plus **$3.95** shipping and handling to:

LightHouse Press
P.O. Box 281375
Nashville, TN 37228

Please allow 2-3 weeks for delivery.